Discoursing with the Beloved

A 40 Day Devotional
Through the Gospel of John

Copyright © 2018
by A.C. Minor

All rights reserved

ISBN-13: 978-1726185936

ISBN-10: 1726185931

Scripture quotations are from the ESV© Bible (The Holy Bible, English Standard Version©), copyright © 2001 by Crossway. Used by permission. All rights reserved.

I dedicate my first book to my first and only love, my beloved wife Carissa Nicole Minor. You will never fully know how much you mean to me and how large of an impact you make on my life.

*Dear heavenly Father, I pray that You use this work as you see fit. If it be to the few or to the many, I ask You to use it for Your glory and for the furtherance of Your kingdom. Use this devotion to show the wicked the joy that they can experience in You.
Amen.*

Contents:

Introduction	11
Day 1: *The Word*	15
Day 2: *The Spirit Descends*	17
Day 3: *Jacob's Ladder*	21
Day 4: *Water into Wine*	23
Day 5: *The Temple*	27
Day 6: *Rebirth*	31
Day 7: *The Baptist's Humility*	33
Day 8: *A Well of Salvation*	35
Day 9: *A Miracle to an Imperfect Faith*	37
Day 10: *Glory Through an Invalid*	41
Day 11: *Mind-belief or Heart-belief*	45
Day 12: *To Whom Shall We Go?*	49
Day 13: *To be Hated*	53
Day 14: *Do Judge Me Correctly*	57
Day 15: *Righteous Rebuke*	59
Day 16: *Avoiding the Truth*	63
Day 17: *Consequential*	67
Day 18: *The Sacrificial Exhibition of Love*	69
Day 19: *The Good Shepherd for all*	73
Day 20: *The Righteous Risk*	75
Day 21: *Believing is not Seeing*	79
Day 22: *The Deadman Witness*	83
Day 23: *It Persists at the Feet*	87
Day 24: *Death to the King!*	91
Day 25: *It Begins with the Feet*	95
Day 26: *Characterized by Love*	99
Day 27: *To Dwell with the Savior*	101
Day 28: *Experiencing the Helper*	103

Day 29: *Pruning for the Harvest*	105
Day 30: *For More than Jewels*	107
Day 31: *He was Emptied so that I may be Filled*	109
Day 32: *Ask for Delight in Me*	113
Day 33: *The Everlasting Intentions of Glory*	117
Day 34: *Joy in the Father*	121
Day 35: *Stop and Dirty Your Knee*	123
Day 36: *The Voice of Truth*	125
Day 37: *To Ordain Thy Death for Thee*	129
Day 38: *The Climax of History*	133
Day 39: *The Risen King*	137
Day 40: *The Restoration*	141
Bibliography	145

Introduction

The Gospel of John is a beautiful account of our Lord Jesus Christ that does not fall into the category of synoptic Gospels. Unlike the synoptic Gospels (Matthew, Mark, and Luke), the Gospel of John possesses a unique structure and theme that the other accounts of Jesus' life, ministry, death, burial, and resurrection do not exhibit to the same degree. I believe this is for a reason. I believe God had a purpose in distinguishing John's Gospel from the other three accounts. For though all four Gospels possess it, John's Gospel has a very heavy emphasis on the truth and beauty of God's infinite and wondrous love.

John, himself, is a unique disciple. God, in His omniscience and infinite wisdom, personally chose John to be a disciple and an apostle. Moreover, for divine reasons, Jesus had a particularly close relationship with John. We find the calling of John as Jesus' disciple in the Gospel of Matthew, where John and his brother James leave their careers as fishermen and their father Zebedee, to follow Jesus in His three-year ministry (Matthew 4:21-23).

John spends three years with the Messiah, witnessing His wondrous and miraculous acts, such as turning water into wine (John 2:1-11), healing a royal official's son (John 4:46-54), healing a paralytic man at the Sheep Gate (John 5:1-17), feeding the five thousand (John 6:1-15), walking on water (John 6:16-21), giving sight to a blind man (John 9), and resurrecting the dead (John 11:38-44).

As did the rest of Jesus' disciples, John was declared apostolic and carried on with the declaration of Jesus' resurrection and His ministry after His ascension. From John, we received four of the 27 books of the New Testament: 1, 2, 3 John and Revelation. In the book of Acts, John accompanied the apostle Peter and received the persecutions and sufferings for their ministry. He was a prominent figure in early church history, no doubt.

John, unlike the rest of the original twelve disciples, did not suffer a horrific death. Instead, he was banished to the island of Patmos, where he received the book of Revelation. According to John Foxe, John was allowed to return from the island of Patmos after the death of the Roman Emperor Domitian and returned to Ephesus where he died around the age of one hundred.[1]

---

[1] John Foxe, *Foxe's Christian Martyrs of the World* (Uchrichsville: Barbour Publishing Inc.), 9-10.

There are many instances in John's Gospel where we find John called "the disciple whom Jesus loved" (John 13:23; 19:26; 21:7; 21:20). We know that it is John that is being referred to when Scripture says, "the disciple whom Jesus loved" because John clearly states this biblical figure as himself in John 21:20-24; but why? Why does Scripture call John "the disciple whom Jesus loved?" Did Jesus not love all of His disciples? Of course, He loved them fervently. However, I believe there is something unique and different about Christ's relationship with the apostle John that made his Gospel stand out and the flavor of his writing attractive.

In Mark 3:17, Jesus calls James and John–the sons of Zebedee–as disciples and gives them an interesting nickname. Jesus gave these two brothers the nickname of "Boanerges," or "Sons of Thunder." "Sons of Thunder" is an interesting nickname because it is quite different from the nickname later ascribed to John–"The Beloved." The online etymological dictionary calls "Beanerges" a "Galilean dialectical corruption of Hebrew bene reghesh 'sons of rage.'"[2] This name characterizes someone who is quick-tempered, tumultuous, overly zealous, negative, impatient, and slow to forgive. To call someone a "Son of Thunder" would not seem to articulate an individual that would write one of the greatest depictions of love that was ever written.

However, that is precisely what God did then, what He does now, and what He will do in the future. He takes people groups and individuals that do not seem adequate for what He has planned and shocks the

---

[2] http://www.etymonline.com/word/boanerges, accessed July 15, 2018.

world with His power through these inadequate specimens.

This seemingly strange behavior of God is precisely what we see in the Gospel of John. For though John starts his encounter with Jesus as a "Son of Thunder," he is very different after three years with the Savior. He becomes closely intimate with the God of the universe. So intimate that he is the only disciple found at the crucifixion scene of Christ (John 19:26-27).

The Gospel of John is an illustrative display and declaration of God's love by a transformed man. Jesus chose an overly zealous man–full of rage–and transformed him to know and exhibit the love of Himself. The great and wonderful Savior of the universe sanctified John so that we would not be discoursing with the Son of Thunder, but we would discourse with the Beloved.

Day 1

The Word

In the beginning was the Word, and the Word was with God, and the Word was God. He was in the beginning with God. All things were made through Him, and without Him was not any thing made that was made. In Him was life, and the life was the light of men. The light shines in the darkness, and the darkness has not overcome it.
John 1:1-5

It should never surprise us that absolutely nothing surprises God. The Bible teaches that God is omniscient, which means He knows everything there is to be known. Nothing resides outside of His all-encompassing knowledge. God never *reacts* to anything. On the contrary, He *pre-acts* to everything.

The crucifixion event of Jesus Christ was not a reaction to evil. Often, we view the sacrifice of Jesus as a reaction to man's union with evil in the garden. God is never caught off guard, and therefore, He knows the ending before the beginning even starts (Isaiah 46:10). The story of the Bible was written to be read backward, from Revelation 22 to Genesis 1.

What does this mean? This realization means that Jesus, the supreme sacrifice for sins, died on the cross before Abraham killed the Ram as a substitute for His son Isaac. This means that Jesus was plan A, not plan

B.[3] This means that the Creator of life in Genesis 1 is also the Giver of life in all of the Gospels!

This means that your holy God has never been oblivious! This means that He had your name written down in the book of life before he even breathed the essence of life into the nostrils of Adam (Revelation 13:10)! This means that your God reigns sovereign and supreme–a force that shackles the gates of hell and melts the padlock of the sinner's chains.

This means that a foreknowing and sovereign God deserves nothing less than our reverence and faith. God knows the outcome of every evil desire and every dependent prayer before it is ever committed or uttered. Trust in the foreknowledge of God, for He knows if you will tomorrow.

I encourage you to read John 1:1-18. These verses of Scripture are called the "Prologue" of the Gospel of John, and it introduces the lovely account of the one Jesus called "the beloved."

---

[3] Robert Smith Jr., *Doctrine that Dances: Bringing Doctrinal Preaching and Teaching to Life* (Nashville: B&H Publishing Group, 2008), 169-170

Day 2

The Spirit Descends

And John bore witness: "I saw the Spirit descend from heaven like a dove, and it remained on Him. I myself did not know Him, but He who sent me to baptize with water said to me, 'He on whom you see the Spirit descend and remain, this is He who baptizes with the Holy Spirit.' And I have seen and have borne witness that this is the Son of God."
John 1:32-34

We receive a more detailed account of Jesus' baptism in the Gospel of Mark (Mark 1:9-11). I encourage you to read the accounts of Jesus' baptism that are in all four Gospels (Matthew 3:13-17; Mark 1:9-11; Luke 3:21-22; John 1:32-34). Why was Jesus, the incarnate God, baptized in the Jordan river? What does that mean for us? Do we have to be baptized to go to heaven? We are sure to find out!

In the days of Noah, water was a negative symbol of judgment and wrath–killing all that inhabited the earth–except for those aboard the ark. After the flood, the symbol of water transitions from a negative symbol of judgment and wrath to a positive symbol of life and grace.

In God's omniscience, He beautifully and wonderfully masterminds His organization of the Bible. The New Testament gazes into God's divine mirror, seeing itself as a beautiful reflection and fulfillment of the Old Testament. Jesus' actions tell the story of the Old Testament! When the Israelites come out of bondage and slavery in Egypt, they *pass through the waters* of the Red Sea and enter the wilderness. Though John does not record the temptation of Jesus, every other Gospel has Jesus going into His time of temptation right after He *passes through the waters* in His baptism. "Where was His temptation event at?" you may ask. His temptation event took place in the wilderness.

If you read the story of the Israelites coming out of Egypt in their pursuit of the promised land, as I encourage you to do, you will find that they always *pass through the waters* to reach a better place on the other side. For example: crossing the Red Sea into liberation from the Egyptians (Exodus 14), the crossing of the Jordan to enter the promised land (Joshua 3), Elijah crossing the Jordon before being taken up into heaven (2 Kings 2:8-12), and Elisha crossing the Jordan, taking up "the spirit of Elijah" (2 Kings 2:13-15).

Baptism is a serious and holy act that portrays the beautiful grace of God. It represents the death, burial, and resurrection of Jesus. When we are been dunked under the water, if held there, death by asphyxiation is inevitable; and we are reminded of the wrath of God during the time of Noah and of Jesus on the Cross.

However, when we have been lifted out of the water, we are also reminded of the grace of God that pulled us out of the wrath that we so justly deserved. Being pushed under the water, we experience the death of the sinful flesh; and by being pulled from the watery depths, we experience God's ark of salvation in new life.

Do we have to be baptized to go to heaven? We shall arrive at our answer when we come to John 3.

Day 3

Jacob's Ladder

Nathaniel answered Him, "Rabbi, you are the Son of God! You are the King of Israel!" Jesus answered him, "Because I said to you, 'I saw you under the fig tree,' do you believe? You will see greater things than these." And He said to him, "Truly, truly, I say to you, you will see heaven opened and the angels of God ascending and descending on the Son of Man."
John 1:49-51

Again, we come to a passage of God's mastery in connecting the New Testament with the Old Testament: "You will see heaven opened and the angels of God ascending and descending on the Son of Man" (vs. 51). In his call of Nathaniel, we receive a beautiful message of who Jesus is.

First, He is alluding to the baptism event that we viewed a few verses earlier in John 1 (see Day 2). The Spirit descending upon Him like a dove was an action showing and stating the deity of Jesus Christ. Jesus was dipped down into the water and burst forth, symbolizing his future resurrection. The heavens split open, and John saw the Spirit of God rest upon Him. Then, a booming voice rang out, "You are my beloved Son, with you I am well pleased" (Mark 1:11).

Second, He alludes to a very significant event in the life of Jacob: "And he dreamed, and behold, there was a ladder set up on the earth, and the top of it reached to heaven. And behold, the angels of God were ascending and descending on it!" (Genesis 28:12). Jesus referred to the event of Jacob's ladder when He spoke to Nathaniel. Why would He mention this random Old Testament story?

For thousands of years the Israelites fervently searched and waited for the Messiah–the "Christos" – to arrive and bring them salvation. Verse upon verse states, describes, and depicts the coming of the Christ figure in Israel. Unfortunately, we do not have the time or space to mention even a sliver of them. However, Jesus is stating here to Nathaniel that He is the Messiah! He is alleging to him that he will see that He is the Christ figure Himself. It is as if He is screaming to Nathaniel, "Nathaniel! I am the ladder connecting earth to heaven!"

There is only one way to salvation–Jesus Christ. Salvation will never come to you by performing good deeds or living an honest life. Salvation will never come to you by being a faithful member of a church body. No matter how many times you kneel at an alter it will never connect you to the Kingdom of God. The only way you will receive salvation is by falling madly in love with Jacob's ladder!

Day 4

Water into Wine

Now there was six stone jars there for the Jewish rites of purification, each holding twenty or thirty gallons. Jesus said to the servants, "Fill the jars with water." And they filled them up to the brim. And he said to them, "Now draw some out and take it to the master of the feast." So they took it. When the master of the feast tasted the water now become wine, and did not know where it came from (though the servants who had drawn the water knew), the master of the feast called the bridegroom and said to him, "Everyone serves the good wine first, and when people have drunk freely, then the poor wine. But you have kept the good wine until now."
John 2:6-10

Turning the water into wine at the wedding at Cana is the first "sign" that John reports in his Gospel. This is a beautiful story about the beginning of Jesus' miraculous three-year ministry. I encourage you to read it all the way through (John 2:1-12). Unfortunately, we do not have the time or space to fully unpack this beautiful work of God like I would like to; but I would like to bring out a couple of realizations.

First, I want us to realize just how big of a deal this miracle was. For my entire childhood, I viewed this historical narrative as a cute little story of Jesus turning some water into wine and everyone thinking it was terrific. It is so much more than that!

I had the privilege and honor of actually visiting Cana in Galilee and seeing stone jars like the ones that held the water Jesus turned into wine. They are massive! I literally stood inside of them![4]

This massive realization was eye-opening for me. Jesus didn't just turn a little pitcher of water into wine. He turned six stone water basins holding twenty to thirty gallons each into wine! That is a colossal amount of wine! But there is more!

Second, I want us to realize just how big of a problem this was for the bridegroom to run out of wine. In the ancient culture, the wedding feast was a huge deal and could last for days. In the middle east, taking care of the guests and providing them with good food is held to the utmost importance. To run out of wine during the wedding feast would be more embarrassing and shameful than we could ever possibly imagine. Jesus not only exhibited His wonder and power as God incarnate, but He also saved the bridegroom from unprecedented amounts of shame and embarrassment.

What is the takeaway? We serve an awesome and almighty God that is gracious and powerful beyond our wildest dreams. It does not matter how deep you bury

---

[4] To see photos of my visit to Cana of Galilee and view jars like the ones Jesus turned water into wine in, visit my Facebook page at https://www.facebook.com/clay.minor.3/media_set?set=a.2267554919927379.1073741834.100000186785657&type=3&uploaded=7

yourself in shame and regret; He can dig you up. Do not fret when you are slammed with hurt and despair. He will use it for His glory. When you run out of wine, and the growl of shame and embarrassment is bearing down on you, remember that God can turn your water into wine–sending shame and embarrassment away with a whimper.

Day 5

The Temple

Jesus answered them, "Destroy this temple, and in three days I will raise it up." The Jews then said, "It has taken forty-six years to build this temple, and will you raise it up in three days?" But he was speaking about the temple of his body.
John 2:19-21

The "cleansing of the temple" is regarded as Jesus' inauguration of His public ministry. I encourage you to read John 2:12-22 to get the full scope of the picture. He strategically waits until the Passover for this inauguration and purposefully kicks it off in the temple.

The temple, historically, has always been a very symbolic and significant fixture in the Jewish community, as well as God's holy Word. When the Israelites came out of bondage from Egypt, God instructed them to build an Ark where God dwelt among His people. There was also a mobile tabernacle built to perform the instructed sacrifices, as they moved about in the wilderness.

There was not a permanent structure built for God to reside among His people until King Solomon had the first temple built. The Babylonians destroyed this temple in approximately 586 B.C.

The House of God was rebuilt around 515 B.C when the governor Nehemiah and the prophet Ezra was commissioned by King Cyrus to rebuild the temple.

Why do I bring up Israeli history? I bring it up because there is a stark and grim difference between Solomon's temple and The Nehemiah/Ezra temple. The difference has overwhelming significance for our inauguration in John chapter two.

When Solomon had the first temple built (1 Kings 6), there was an interesting element that the Nehemiah/Ezra temple was void of–the presence of God! The Ark was brought into the temple and Scripture says, "And when the priests came out of the Holy Place, a cloud filled the house of the LORD, so that the priests could not stand to minister because of the cloud, for the glory of the LORD filled the house of the LORD." (1 Kings 8:10-11). God's presence was among His people.

We never find this crucial aspect in the Nehemiah/Ezra temple. They finish, dedicate, and offer sacrifices at the rebuilt temple (Ezra 6). Ezra reads the law of Moses at the rebuilt temple (Nehemiah 8). They confess their sins (Nehemiah 9; Ezra 10), and they declare a renewing covenant (Nehemiah 10), but the glory of the LORD never enters the rebuilt temple. There is no Ark. There is no Cloud. There is no glory. Furthermore, God declares His silence to His people in Malachi 4:5-6.

It appeared as though God had vanished; as if He had ducked away to His heavenly throne never to be seen or heard from again. But then, from the lineage of David, there was a baby boy born in a manger in Bethlehem; and God "showed up" again!

Jesus went to the temple that day, drove out the money changers with a cord, and declared that He would raise Himself up on the third day–to proclaim His divinity. He proclaimed to a blind and deaf people that He was God almighty, and the Savior they had been waiting thousands of years for.

Do not be blind and deaf today, for we are the temple that God is to fill with a Cloud to shine His excellent glory! Let Him in, because He rose again on the third day! By the way, the rebuilt temple was destroyed by the Romans in 70 A.D. and has yet to be rebuilt.

Day 6

Rebirth

Jesus answered, "Truly, truly, I say unto you, unless one is born of water and the Spirit, he cannot enter the kingdom of God. That which is born of the flesh is flesh, and that which is born of the Spirit is spirit."
John 3:5-6

The interesting encounter with the Pharisee named Nicodemus is where we get our favorite salvation verse in John 3:16. I encourage you to read the entire Nicodemus encounter (John 3:1-21). Jesus speaks to a Pharisee concerning something he should already know–how to enter into the kingdom of God. We would term their conversation today as a salvation rich introduction to the Gospel. Jesus clearly spelled out to Nicodemus the way to salvation–the way to the Kingdom of the Father.

Jesus tells him, "And as Moses lifted up the serpent in the wilderness, so must the Son of Man be lifted up, that whoever believes in him may have eternal life." (John 3:14-15). Jesus alluded to the Old Testament occurrence when God sent venomous snakes among the Israelites to punish and remind them of their garden like rebellion (Numbers 21). Nicodemus, being a fervent student of the law, would undoubtedly be familiar with this story.

Just as the cure for their venomous snake bite was to gaze upon the bronze snake high on the pole, Jesus lifted up on His pole–the cross–is our cure to the deadly bite of sin. Thus, we get a beautiful and masterful presentation of the Gospel from our Lord. However, Jesus also answers a tense theological debate in this encounter.

Do we have to be baptized to enter the kingdom of God? Yes, absolutely yes (Mark 16:16)! However, by what means do we speak of when we declare that a man or woman must be baptized to enter into heaven? To enter into the kingdom of God, we must be baptized by the Holy Spirit, not merely dunked in water. This means that the God of all the universe must come and dwell within our souls. Salvation is not merely believing in Christ's existence or even the existence of his obedient acts. But rather, it is being transformed by His existence–a Holy Spirit infiltration of our soul. It is the rebirth of the Holy Spirit that saves our souls, and it is the Holy Spirit that will lift us up to meet Jesus in the air.

Day 7

The Baptist's Humility

"You yourselves bear me witness, that I said, 'I am not the Christ, but I have been sent before him.' The one who has the bride is the bridegroom. The friend of the bridegroom, who stands and hears him, rejoices greatly at the bridegroom's voice. Therefore this joy of mine is now complete. He must increase, but I must decrease."
John 3:28-30

John the Baptist has always been one of my favorite characters in the Bible. Here, we see a glimpse of why Jesus declared him the greatest of those born of women (Matthew 11:11). John the Baptist exhibits beautiful and radical humility. He spends twelve verses exalting Christ (John 3:22-36). A tense situation arises where Jesus' ministry begins to grow larger than John the Baptist's. Instead of growing bitter like his disciples, his exuberant humility shines as he places the standings in the correct ranking.

He understands that his role as the paver of the way is coming to an end, and he must "decrease so Jesus can increase." Just as Abraham humbly set his authoritative role aside to give Lot the first shot at the land before them (Genesis 13:8-12), John lays his power of influence down for the One whose sandal strap he is unworthy to untie (John 1:26).

Deeply embedded in all sin is the infectious seed of pride. Pride is what tainted the heart of Satan, casting him down from the throngs of heaven (Ezekiel 28). Within the soul of all mankind resides the self-exalting pride that expels us from the kingdom of God. It was in the garden that we decided to make ourselves a god (Genesis 3). All pride is the attempt to thrust ourselves above the sovereign will and authority of God.

We often make the mistake of viewing humility as caring more for others than we do ourselves. Though it is true that we should care for others more than ourselves, such a statement of humility is incomplete. True humility is not merely caring more for others, but submitting entirely to God, such as John the Baptist.

I have known several individuals who were humble in the sense that they did many works of philanthropy, yet they cared nothing for the glory and the will of the Father. Such a view of humility is incomplete because when we totally submit to the Father, caring for others simply falls into the suit. We love and do for others because Christ first loved and died for us.

Where do you reside in this manner? Are you humble? Be careful! For Satan dwells within incorrect assumptions of righteousness. Are you submitted entirely to God? Or are you living life for yourself? You can correctly judge your heart by the actions that it produces. Do you tithe? Or do you spend your stolen money on yourself? Do you go to a worship service? Or do you sleep in on Sunday because "It is the only day that you have to spend with the family?"

Walk humbly Christian; for it is pride that will take Christ out of your name. May our hearts sing, "I must decrease so He may increase."

Day 8

A Well of Salvation

Jesus said to her, "Everyone who drinks this water will be thirsty again, but whoever drinks of the water that I will give him will never be thirsty again. The water that I will give him will become in him a spring of water welling up to eternal life."
John 4:13-14

The story of the woman at the well is one of the most beautiful stories in all of the Bible. In this story, we get to see the Master Evangelist share the Gospel with a weary and broken soul. I encourage you to read the story of the woman at the well in its entirety (John 4:1-42). There are many things that we can glean from this wonderful and peculiar story.

First, we find our Lord using Old Testament language when He says, "The water that I will give him will become in him a spring of water welling up to eternal life" (vs. 14). The divine thirst quench that Jesus gives us in His saving grace is never-ending. When the ravaged wicked soul, plagued by misery, is filled with the lifesaving riches of God's amazing grace, he is filled with an eternity of unmeasurable joy and pleasure that will never cease. Like an eternal river, no drought can squelch out the moistures of His perfect love and beauty in the heart of the believer.

Second, this passage of wonder and encouragement also comes with a stern charge. In Matthew's Gospel Jesus tells us that we are to be the salt of the earth (Matthew 5:13). If we are to be the salt of the earth, we should also inherit the thirst provoking element of salt.

When a desperate world looks at a born-again believer, it should not look into a mirror, seeing its reflection of wickedness. Instead, it should see a desirable joy and separation that causes it to thirst for the source of that joy and separation. If we are to cause the world to thirst by our saltiness, we also are to display the relieving answer to their parchment–Jesus' living water.

When Jesus spoke with the woman at the well, their conversation sparked a movement in her town that left it changed, never to be the same again. God's mission is displayed for His children to see: "The fields are ripe for harvest" (John 4:35). It is the responsibility of His children to fulfill His mission by parching the world with their saltiness and presenting the quench of their souls with His living water.

Day 9

A Miracle to an Imperfect Faith

When this man heard that Jesus had come from Judea to Galilee, he went to him and asked him to come down and heal his son, for he was at the point of death. So Jesus said to him, "Unless you see signs and wonders you will not believe." The official said to him, "Sir, come down before my child dies." Jesus said to him, "Go; your son will live." The man believed the word that Jesus spoke to him and went on his way.
John 4:47-50

As we come to the second "sign" of Jesus in the Gospel account of John, I urge you to pay close attention to how it plays out. We come upon the healing of an official's son who is deathly sick. I encourage you to read this second sign in its entirety (John 4:46-54), as well as the three verses before that impact it (John 4:43-45).

Jesus leaves Judea and enters into Galilee declaring that a prophet has no honor in his hometown; for they would not believe in Him there (John 4:43-44). Jesus enters into Galilee a discovered and famous man–producing quite the different atmosphere. These people have heard of the mighty and wonderful works that Jesus has done; they wish to see it for themselves.

Galilee is where Jesus performed His first sign (turning water into wine), and they crave to see something spectacular. Therefore, it is not long before someone in genuine need approaches Jesus and requests the mighty miracles everyone has heard of. And here lies the issue with the people of Jesus' second sign.

There is no doubt that these people (the official in particular) had some form of belief or faith in Jesus, but something is lacking. Jesus Himself tells the official, "Unless you see signs and wonders you will not believe" (vs. 48).

These people, this man, begin with an imperfect faith. Imperfect faith produces one of two outcomes: a doubting and rebellious heart (we will see this on a grand scale in John 6), or a beautiful submission and transformation of trust.

Here we see the latter. The official goes home, finds his son miraculously healed, and he and his whole household believe. They make the transition from a damnable, imperfect, watered down, lukewarm faith, to a brilliant, transforming, all-consuming faith of saving grace.

I cannot begin to express how many people I have come into contact with that claimed they would believe in Jesus if He would "just give them a sign." Unfortunately, I fear that most of these people fall into the same pitiful category as the blind people of John 6– they would not see a sign from God if it clapped with an angelic boom, split the heavenly skies, and shown a brilliant light onto their woeful and tight shut eyes.

Therefore, with this in mind, it does cause one to press upon the reason of their own personal belief. Why do we go to church, sing songs of praise, raise our hands in submission, and believe upon the name of Jesus Christ? Is it because we have heard that He has done beautiful and wonderful works, and so, we follow after the hype and reputation of the Savior? Or is it because our veil of blindness has been lifted; and a performed miracle or not, our hearts and souls have been transformed to factually believe upon the Savior in whom we have never laid our eyes upon? We are tempted to hastily choose the answer with the good outcome, but honesty may save your soul. Where do you remain–imperfect faith or submissive trust?

Day 10

Glory Through an Invalid

One man was there who had been an invalid for thirty-eight years. When Jesus saw him lying there and knew that he had already been there a long time, he said to him, "Do you want to be healed?" The sick man answered him, "Sir, I have no one to put me into the pool when the water is stirred up, and while I am going another steps down before me." Jesus said to him, "Get up, take up your bed, and walk." And at once the man was healed, and he took up his bed and walked.
John 5:5-10

This sign of our Lord, as with all of His signs, was purposed to bring divinity to Himself and glory to the Father on high. Jesus' central goal in everything He did was to usher people to the glory of the heavenly Father. He selflessly humbled Himself, even to a cross (Philippians 2:5-11), to obediently fulfill the will and glory of the Creator of the universe. Our Lord was purposeful and wonderful; this occasion is no exception.

The poor soul that lay by the pool at the sheep gate was truly a victim of his circumstances and his time. He was an outcast of society–stricken with crippling sickness with no one to care for him. He was considered useless–nothing to offer to his people or culture. He was doomed within the pit of failure, and destined for certain death. His sad fate was sealed, and hope for his salvation was nowhere to be found. This invalid was like many others that went before him–helpless. This was his reality until the King of kings and Lord of lords strolled into town.

An interesting difference between this invalid and the official with a dying son (John 4:47-50) should be noticed: the invalid never approached the Savior as the official did. He never asked for help, salvation, redemption, healing, or anything. He never even called out to Jesus as He came into the town.

Instead, our Lord made the initiative and approached this destitute soul and asked him, "Do you want to be healed?" (vs. 6). It was our Lord that told him, "Get up, take your bed, and walk" (vs. 8). It was our Lord that approached him later to offer counsel (John 5:14). What's the purpose? The implications for this stark reality are beautiful and wonderful.

When we are within the depths of calamity, it will do us a world of benefit to understand the purpose of our tragedy. God is sovereign over all, including our woes and trials. Just as God was in total control of Satan's sifting of Job, ready and able to halt Satan's aspirations at any given moment, He is in complete control of our situational calamity. Why would God subject His children to worldly horrors? He would subject His children to them for many reasons, but ultimately it would be overwhelmingly for the same central reason our poor invalid was crippled at the pool of the sheep gate–for God's glory!

Jesus sought after this hopeless Jew to exhibit His remarkable healing power. The reasons and answers for our poverty are no different. Whether it is to display His healing power upon our woeful spirit, or to prove the endurance of His children, our trials and tribulations will always begin, persist, and conclude with the glory of the Father!

Day 11

Mind-belief or Heart-belief

Then they said to him, "What must we do, to be doing the works of God?" Jesus answered them, "This is the work of God, that you believe in him whom he has sent." So they said to him, "Then what sign do you do, that we may see and believe you? What work do you perform? Our fathers ate the manna in the wilderness; as it is written, 'He gave them bread from heaven to eat.'"
John 6:28-31

Here, in John chapter six, we see an opposite transition from the imperfect faith we saw in the Official in John chapter four (reread Day 9 to refresh your memory). I strongly urge you to read chapter six in its entirety for you to grasp the gravity of our current text.

Once again, we begin with a people who initially have a degree of faith–they followed Jesus all the way to Capernaum, seeking Him out. These are the same people who sat on a grassy hillside and witnessed Jesus feed them with two loaves of bread and two fish. These are the same people who had to travel to the other side of the sea because our Lord walked across it. Just as the spectators in Cana "believed" in him because of His miracles (John 4), these people also "believe" in Him only for His miracles. He miraculously filled them at supper, and now they desire a miraculous breakfast.

Faith can never be removed from genuine belief–the two are married and cannot be divorced. However, there are two types of very different belief. I call them mind-belief and heart-belief. They hold a fine line and involve enormous implications for the soul's eternal outcome. One involves supernatural satisfaction, while the other involves ongoing discontent. One involves wholehearted submission and trust, while the other involves doubt and disillusionment. One involves eternal security, while the other involves eternal damnation.

Almost every human being possesses at least some degree of mind-belief. This is why 89% of Americans say they believe in God.[5] However, if the essence of your faith in Christ contains only mind-belief, you are no different than Satan; for mind-belief isn't supernatural. Satan believes in God. Satan believes in Jesus. Satan even believes that Jesus came to die on a cross for sins and rose from the grave three days later. However, Satan will not inherit the Kingdom of God. This is why James said, "You believe that God is one; you do well. Even the demons believe–and shudder!" (James 2:19). This is where most of the five thousand remains. After Jesus fully explains to them who He is– the Son of God offering eternal life–they depart from Him (John 6:66). It is frightening to think that we could be fed by the hand of God and completely miss out on His true purpose.

---

[5] Michael Lipka, "Americans' faith in God may be eroding," http://www.pewresearch.org/fact-tank/2015/11/04/americans-faith-in-god-may-be-eroding/, accessed on July 4, 2018.

The individual with heart-belief will never be concerned with the need for a miracle; because he is totally and wholly overwhelmed by the miracle that transformed his soul. Mind-belief finds its essence in knowledge; while heart-belief finds its essence in experiential transformation. Don't waste your life watching the works and miracles of God, only to miss who He truly is. For when we come to the end of our days and approach judgment, God will be less interested in how much we know than how much we experienced.

Day 12

To Whom Shall We Go?

After this many of his disciples turned back and no longer walked with him. So Jesus said to the Twelve, "Do you want to go away as well?" Simon Peter answered him, "Lord, to whom shall we go? You have the words of eternal life, and we have believed, and have come to know, that you are the Holy One of God."
John 6:66-69

Due to his many thoughtless and careless moments throughout the Gospels, I like to call Simon Peter "Big Mouth Peter." As you proceed through the story of the Gospels, you almost wince every time Peter says something irreverent, uneducated, or downright ignorant, knowing the rebuke of the Son is not far away. To Peter's defense, he was largely the voice of the disciples, and therefore, many times took the blame for what everyone else was already pondering and thinking.

However, here, at the tail end of the sixth chapter, we are presented with one of the most beautiful and revealing questions in all of the Bible. If "Big Mouth Peter" ever got it right, it was when he uttered the humble response of, "Lord, to whom shall we go? You have the words of eternal life, and we have believed, and have come to know, that you are the Holy One of God" (vs. 68-69).

The Gospel of Jesus Christ is repulsive and offensive to those gripped by the bondage of the world. This is why when Jesus presents it to the multitudes of people here in chapter six–explaining that eternal life rests entirely and exclusively in Him–many turns away and no longer follow Him. They declare Jesus' Gospel "too hard" (John 6:60) and begin to grumble amongst themselves. So, are they correct? Is Jesus' Gospel rather difficult? I would say yes.

Here, we stumble across one of the many interesting and beautiful paradoxes of the Bible: Jesus' Gospel is the easiest difficulty that mankind has ever experienced. I scorn those who distastefully describe the Gospel as an earthly route to luxury and fortune–describing salvation as an instant solution to all of your sinful desires and earthly woes.

When I read the chapters of the New Testament, luxury and bliss is not the story and reality that I find within its pages. On the contrary, I find men who continually attempt to fight off their sinful desires (Romans 7:15-20), and men who experience inevitable persecution of unimaginable proportions (1 Peter 4:12-19). Historically, accepting the Gospel has produced a bloody miserable experience. However, it is also that very Gospel that turns a bloody miserable experience into a joyful persevering life (James 1:2-4). What is the point? How does this tie to Peter's question?

God is a jealous God that is not interested in acquiring a half-hearted Christian. His Gospel is an all or nothing deal–He wants you in or out. He has no taste for those who religiously blaspheme His name by straddling the fence (Revelation 3:15-16). Therefore, God strips His children bear and naked, to utilize the refining fires of suffering, to clothe us with His skins of holiness. Jesus said to deny ourselves and take up our cross (Luke 9:23). He desires for us to cast our comforts and cushions into the fires of hell where they belong, so that, when the temptations of doubt and abandonment arise and ask us to walk away from our Savior, we may humbly inquire, "Lord, to whom shall we go?"

Day 13

To be Hated

So his brothers said to him, "Leave here and go to Judea, that your disciples also may see the works you are doing. For no one works in secret if he seeks to be known openly. If you do these things, show yourself to the world." For not even his brothers believed in him. Jesus said to them, "My time has not yet come, but your time is always here. The world cannot hate you, but it hates me because I testify about it that its works are evil.
John 7:3-7

In the Gospel of Matthew, Jesus states that He came not to bring peace into the world, but a sword–turning the members of a household into enemies (Matthew 10:34-36). This is personified better nowhere else than here in John's seventh chapter. The text says, "For not even his brothers believed in him" (vs. 5). Jesus was bold and outspoken; and unfortunately, He didn't line up with what His brothers expected or wanted out of Him. Jesus and His brothers had adverse motives.

It is a heartbreaking tragedy when the relationship between a father and son, mother and daughter, or the relationship between siblings is shattered. However, it is also a beautiful exhibition of sold-out faith when one chooses Jesus over a tight-knit family relationship.

This is beautiful because Jesus also said, "Whoever loves father or mother more than me is not worthy of me, and whoever loves son or daughter more than me is not worthy of me. And whoever does not take his cross and follow me is not worthy of me" (Matthew 10:37-38). Jesus selflessly exhibited the reality that a relationship with the Creator is fundamentally far greater in importance than human relationships, even the closest ones.

Why did Jesus and His brothers have adverse motives? Jesus' brothers were consumed with the infectious disease of worldly pride. They wished to be the brothers of the promised Messiah–the Savior of Israel. Where Jesus had eyes for Fatherly glory, sacrifice, salvation, and humility, they had eyes for self-glory, fame, money, and power. They were not hated by the world that so hated their divine Brother because they were intimately woven into the fabric of its essence! The world burned passionately for them because they burned passionately for the world!

What about us? Does the world hate us? Or does it race with the emotion of fervency at the thought of our presence? John Piper so truthfully said, "The world does not need cool Christians who are culturally saturated. It needs exiles with the scent of heaven and the aroma of Christ."[6] Are you hated because you smell like what the world so desperately needs? Or are you beloved because you lack the smell that the world so detestably hates? In the third chapter of Revelation, Jesus says He will vomit the lukewarm Christian out of

---

[6] John Piper, https://twitter.com/johnpiper/status/836924308505133058?lang=en, accessed July 4, 2018.

His mouth (Revelation 3:16). Do you carry the sweet aroma of Jesus Christ? Or do you smell like vomit?

Day 14

Do Judge Me Correctly

"If on the Sabbath a man receives circumcision, so that the law of Moses may not be broken, are you angry with me because on the Sabbath I made a man's whole body well? Do not judge by appearances, but judge with right judgement."
John 7:23-24

The Jews were still disgruntled by Jesus' healing of the invalid in chapter five (see Day 10). The Scribes and the Pharisees were so love struck with the law that they failed to see and understand the miraculous acts of the Maker of the law. Jesus would later declare their death in sin and their future denial into the kingdom of God (John 7:33-34). Jesus would also state that the Sabbath was made for man, not man for the Sabbath–establishing Himself Lord over the Sabbath (Mark 2:23-28). If Jesus–God almighty incarnate–wishes to heal a man on the Sabbath, no one is to stop Him. Then, Jesus utters an interesting statement: "Do not judge by appearances, but judge with right judgement" (vs. 24).

I would like to point out first what Jesus did not say. He did not say, "Never ever judge." Instead, He urged the Jews to judge with correct judgment, due to their legalistic squabbling concerning His healing of a man on the Sabbath. There is a very distinct difference between, "Do not judge," and "Judge correctly."

Human beings detest having their inconsistencies singled out by another individual. It is the pride within us that insists on asserting we are correct in everything we do. This is why our society barks, "Do not judge me! You do not know me to judge me!"

Interestingly, the vast majority of people who bark such a fallacy do not want a neutral judgment. They do not want you to give them a fair assessment. Instead, they wish for you to judge them positively, regardless of their prior actions; and therefore, they become disgruntled when you "judge" them reasonably based upon your observations.

If you take the opportunity to study the verses of Scripture concerning righteous judgment, the number of verses relating to the subject is overwhelming. I encourage you to investigate the many Old Testament and New Testament verses involving the aspect of rebuking a brother. Unfortunately, we do not have the time or space to unpack righteous judgment (it would take a full-sized book to do it justice).

However, I believe we can glean the same central idea that Jesus points out to the Jews: judge correctly. Judgment is to be done gently, thoughtfully, understandably, and without impeding upon divine judgment–salvation. Judge correctly to guard your heart, mind, and soul; but do not judge by appearances alone.

Day 15

Righteous Rebuke

And as they continued to ask him, he stood up and said to them, "Let him who is without sin among you be the first to throw a stone at her." And once more he bent down and wrote on the ground.
John 8:7-8

I must begin by recognizing that our particular text in use (John 7:53-8:11) is disputed by many holy and righteous biblical scholars in regards to its validity, due to its absence in the most ancient manuscripts and to its inconsistent placement in the manuscripts that do include it. Though I do find many of their arguments valid, the story of the woman caught in adultery resonates with the beauty and character of our Savior, and therefore, it should be highly valued. I encourage you to read the entire encounter (John 7:53-8:11).

The scribes and the Pharisees attempt, yet again, to trip up and confuse the Master–the very essence of wisdom and knowledge. And, yet again, they fall flat on their face. They bring a complicated situation to Jesus with the desired purpose of enabling the people to see who they think He truly is–a "foolish fraud." However, He does nothing but shows how magnificently gracious and authentic He truly is.

It is important to note that by Mosaic law, Jesus really could have legally stoned this woman. However, in doing so, He would have broken the Roman law that reserved capital punishment for the Roman officials.

The central point that I would like to make, and what Jesus masterfully brings out Himself, is that to judge someone of their sin you must be pure from sin yourself. Please understand that there is a vast difference in judging sin for eternity (God's job) and rebuking your brother or sister who has fallen into sin (our job). What Jesus showed to the scribes and Pharisees is that they were totally unfit and unqualified for either.

We must not be ignorant, as the scribes and Pharisees were, and miss Jesus' words when He said, "First take the log out of your own eye, and then you will see clearly to take the speck out of your brother's eye" (Matthew 7:5). If we are going to perform the God-given duty of tenderly rebuking our brothers and sisters in Christ, we must first make sure we are not victims of sin ourselves. It would make no sense for you to charge a raging alcoholic to put down the booze, all while taking shots yourself. It would be ridiculous for you to plead with a thief to pay for the things he steals, all while you slip the latest and greatest gadget into your pocket. It would be a tragedy for you to urge the adulterer to set his mind upon the Lord, all while you view inappropriate materials on your computer. It would be hypocritical for you to tell the liar to speak the truth, all while you gossip about others behind their back. We cannot dishonor God's name by committing the sins we charge against the world.

Sin is a ravenous creature that inflicts great destruction upon those it leeches onto. It is our duty, as soldiers of Christ, to lovingly rebuke those who follow its lure. However, make sure you process your lumber before you go speck hunting; and seek purity before you seek to cast stones.

Day 16

Avoiding the Truth

"You are of your father the devil, and your will is to do your father's desires. He was a murderer from the beginning, and does not stand on the truth, because there is no truth in him. When he lies, he speaks out of his own character, for he is a liar and the father of lies. But because I tell the truth, you do not believe me. Which one of you convicts me of sin? If I tell the truth, why do you not believe me? Whoever is of God hears the words of God. The reason why you do not hear them is that you are not of God."
John 8:44-47

I detested my four years of high school with every fiber of my being. "This will be the best four years of your life!" they said. Nope. The years that I have lived post-graduation have been infinitely greater. Yes, I made some fantastic lifelong friends in high school, in whom I will treasure forever, but overall it was a miserable experience.

I believe high school was grueling for me because it is almost entirely void of truth. In school, life consists of getting ahead, acting cool, and making good impressions–all in the name of popularity. Teenagers will lie, steal, and cheat to impress the correct people–at precisely the right time–to get the desired response. High School is a showcase of deception and rivalry–void of love and truth. Unfortunately, after high school, I found that it was no different in "big boy world." Lie, steal, and cheat, is the name of the game; and you better watch out!

The Pharisees could not have been a more picture-perfect example of a 21st-century high school–utterly deceptive with a flamboyant lust for popularity. Jesus was gracious enough to reveal the path to eternal life to them, as He had multiple times, and they would not have it. Self-images and "upholding tradition" literally caused them to pick up stones to kill the very Son of God! Their immense desire to uphold the law and make an impressive impression gave them the title of sons of the devil–not of God.

It doesn't matter where you go in the world, this unfortunate truth–denial of the truth–is pervasive. This is why the Bible has continued to maintain its relevancy for thousands of years–it deals with the same condition of mankind generation after generation. Further troubling is the fact that this pervasive denial of the truth does not reserve itself to the outside of the church building. It wriggles and shifts until it seeps its way into the church's cracks, bringing the stench of hell with it.

Who is your father? Is he heavenly or damnable? If you find that your heart is consumed with deception and the lust to "fit in," beware of your soul. If you are more in control of your life than the God you claim to have a relationship with, beware of your soul. If you are honest with yourself, and your heart does not align with the commands of our Savior, beware of your soul.

I invite you to come out of the bondage of your sins, and rest in the words of our Lord when He says, "If you abide in my word, you are truly my disciples, and you will know the truth, and the truth will set you free" (John 8:31-32).

Day 17

Consequential

As he passed by, he saw a man blind from birth. And his disciples asked him, "Rabbi, who sinned, this man or his parents, that he was born blind? Jesus answered, "It was not that this man sinned, or his parents, but that the works of God might be displayed in him. We must work the works of him who sent me while it is day; night is coming, when no one can work. As long as I am in the world, I am the light of the world."
John 9:1-5

There will always be a detrimental cost to sin. When we create an idol out of ourselves, heeding to the commands of our own pleasure and neglecting the commands of the Father, we heap fiery coals of consequence onto our lives. However, the consequence of sin does not always come in a physical form. In fact, it is when a woeful sinner realizes the harshest implication of sin–that with each committed sin he steps further and further away from the Father–that he actually deals with his sin issue.

Here, in the healing of the blind man, Jesus answers this puzzling question of His disciples, concerning the source of his physical blindness.

There certainly can be a physical consequence of sinful actions. There are several instances of it throughout scripture, such as Cain's curse and banishment for murdering his brother Abel (Genesis 4:11-16), God withholding Moses' entry into the promised land (Numbers 20:12), the death of David's son born by Bathsheba (2 Samuel 12:15-18), etc. However, the Pharisees took the idea of physical consequence to a heretical level, declaring anyone with a physical defect to be under God's curse because of their wickedness.

Jesus makes it very clear that neither the blind man's sin nor his parent's sin, was the source of his blindness from birth. Jesus wishes to change the incorrect mindset of his disciples. When others gripped with misfortune, pain, and suffering pass before us, it should not cause us to question the source of the disability ignorantly; but rather, it should charge us to the action of servanthood and compassion. Our chance to be available for the opportunities of God are here only for a short time. It is our responsibility to partake in them.

Are you available for the works of God to be displayed in you? Our sole purpose in existing in the universe is to bring God glory (Isaiah 43:6-7). May our prayer be for God to exhibit and manifest His glory through us supernaturally.

God does not need your wants, wishes, or even your talents; He desires your availability. God provides the resources and abilities to those who obediently step out in faith to be subjects of His glory. What about you? Are you available for God to display His works through you? Or are you too busy for Him to even make an appointment to see you?

Day 18

The Sacrificial Exhibition of Love

"The thief comes only to steal and kill and destroy. I came that they may have life and have it abundantly. I am the good shepherd. The good shepherd lays down his life for the sheep."
John 10:10-11

I have often heard that if love could be summed up in one word, that word would be "give." Those we truly have love and compassion for are those in whom we pour ourselves out to in sacrifice. In the ideal marital cycle, you have two individuals who care more for each other than they do themselves, continually giving and sacrificing for the other's wellbeing. There is no higher or supreme example of the giving sacrificial definition of love than that of our Lord and Savior, Jesus Christ.

It is widely known how tumultuously the Pharisees treated Jesus of Nazareth, but in their defense, Jesus was not the first "Messiah" to arrive on the scene in Jerusalem that they had to deal with. If you look back through Jewish history, you will find multiple unanointed individuals who claimed messianic authority. This is why Jesus says in the verses prior, "All who came before me are thieves and robbers, but the sheep did not listen to them" (John 10:8). All of the individuals claiming to be the Messiah, prior to Jesus, had one crucial difference from Jesus in common: they did not fulfill the giving sacrificial definition of love.

On the contrary, Jesus calls them, "Thieves and robbers." To them, the position of Messiah was a position of power, greed, and persuasion. The false messiahs came to corruptly gain, and the true Messiah–Jesus Christ–came to give life and give it abundantly.

There are two things that I want us to see here. First and foremost, we need to look at just how giving and sacrificial our Savior was and is. Hanging on the cross was not only a mere weekend business trip for our God. Instead, it was the crime of all history, resulting in the death of His Son. Jesus died so that we may live!

Not only that, but Jesus gave His life for sinners that deserved nothing more than hellfire and brimstone. Let us not forget that without the one true Messiah we would be gnashing our teeth in that horrific environment where the worm never dies. We owe absolutely every aspect of our being to the one who supremely gave it all.

Secondly, I want us to see, comprehend, and heed Christ's definition of love. I wonder how often we love those around us the way Jesus loves–with a giving and sacrificial spirit. A Godly relationship is not an iron-fisted brute of a man who rules oppressively over the woman; nor is it a domineering woman who "hen pecks" or "whips her man into shape." A Godly relationship is a relationship that finds its root in the love of Christ.

Do you love those around you as Jesus loves? Do you sacrificially give, being the picture of Jesus to those around you? Or do you selfishly take from everyone who doesn't notice that you are a thief and a robber?

Day 19

The Good Shepherd for all

"I am the good shepherd. I know my own and my own know me, just as the Father knows me and I know the Father; and I lay down my life for the sheep. And I have other sheep that are not of this fold. I must bring them also, and they will listen to my voice. So there will be one flock, one shepherd. For this reason the Father loves me, because I lay down my life that I may take it up again."
John 10:14-17

The idea of a coming Messiah is not a New Testament idea. In fact, the third chapter of Genesis is where we first get a glimpse of a coming Savior (Genesis 3:14-15). The Old Testament is saturated with the prophecies of a Messiah that will make everything just and holy again. However, it is evident throughout the Old Testament that the coming Savior would be of the Jews. Jesus validifies this when he speaks to the woman at the well in John chapter four: "You worship what you do not know; we worship what we know, for salvation is from the Jews" (John 4:22).

Jesus of Nazareth, born of the Virgin Mary and of the lineage of David, is the answer to these ancient prophecies. He is born of Jewish descent and ushers in salvation to the Jews. He calls His disciples: Simon

Peter, Andrew, James son of Zebedee, John, Philip, Bartholomew, Thomas, Matthew, James son of Alphaeus, Thaddaeus (Nathaniel), Simon the Zealot, and Judas Iscariot–all of Jewish descent. He spends His three-year ministry proclaiming salvation to the Jewish people. He hangs upon a cross, spilling His blood for the cleansing of sins on Mount Calvary, which is the capital of Jerusalem. Salvation began with the Jewish people.

Praise God, however, that the story does not end with the Jewish people! For though salvation began with the Jewish people, it does not end within the borders of the land of Israel. We (the Gentiles), are the "other sheep that are not of this fold" (vs. 16).

Jesus charged His disciples on the day of His ascension to heaven with the command to proclaim the ground-breaking truth of the Gospel to the outer ends of the earth (Acts 1:8). Due to the Holy Spirit's inspiration of the apostle Paul and the disciples, the Gospel has reached the outer ends of the globe. You and I, as descendants of pagan people, may be called sons and daughters of the highest God.

Take the time today to reflect on the superlative grace of God. Let your body shake, your eyes stream with tears, and let your heart pound with reverence as you contemplate on the mercy of the Savior.

Spend time in prayer thanking God for laying His life down for the sheep of the other fold–the pagan gentiles. Bow down in the dirt as you contemplate the redemption of your sin, in awe and adoration. Then, get up, dust yourself off, and serve the King. For you have a life to give and a ministry to partake in, all because of the Grace of the suffering Servant.

Day 20

The Righteous Risk

Then Jesus told them plainly, "Lazarus has died, and for your sake I am glad that I was not there, so that you may believe. But let us go to him." So Thomas, called the Twin, said to his fellow disciples, "Let us also go, that we may die with him."
John 11:14-16

Fear is one of the most influential and most debilitating emotions of the human spirit. After the fervent passions of love, the intense effects of fear rests as the number two most impactful realities of the human psyche. If we are not careful, we will let fear overrun our aspirations and dreams, leaving us to regretfully ask, "What if?" Entirely more critical, fear can also prevent us from being obedient to the Father and keep us from experiencing His beautiful acts of provision.

Here in the eleventh chapter of John, Jesus is suggesting they go back to Judea to raise Lazarus from the dead. The disciples are torn. They love Lazarus dearly and wish to see him resurrected, but they are equally stricken with fear to enter the land of Judea. Practically speaking, going to Judea is not a good idea. Jesus is not a famous rock star among the religious leaders of Judea. Instead, He is the face posted on the "Wanted

Dead or Alive" posters. They know that traveling to Judea will not be without its consequences.

The disciples have a reverent respect for Jesus and possess a relatively strong belief in Him. They honestly do believe in Jesus; for they are willing to travel to Judea and die alongside Him. However, their faith in Jesus is not yet complete. They know Jesus well enough to listen to Him and enter into the valley of the shadow of death, but they still lack the intimacy needed to believe that Jesus can save them from the grips of the Judeans.

They possess a blind faith–they believe enough to follow Him, but not enough to trust in Him. What enables this hesitation to bridge over to full submission? The barrier that prevents us from fully trusting in the Savior is fear–fear of the unknown. When you break the barrier of fear, hesitation transforms into submission.

I do not know what God has specifically called you to. However, I can almost guarantee that whatever God is calling you to do, it is risky. The mountain movers throughout history–those who performed mighty works for the Lord–were risk takers in righteousness. God makes his plan risky for a purpose; that is what faith is all about.

It's not that God wants you to take a shot and hope everything works out–that is the blind faith approach that once consumed Thomas. Instead, God wants you to obediently step out in faith, take a righteous risk, and know that He has got you. This doesn't mean your risk will not come without pain, suffering, or consequence; but it does mean God will proudly smile at the obedient actions of His faithful servant. Find out what God is calling you to do, step out in faith, and take a risk. The Father is beckoning to do something wild and amazing! Will you risk it all for Him?

Day 21

Believing is not Seeing

Now when Mary came to where Jesus was and saw him, she fell at his feet, saying to him, "Lord, if you had been here, my brother would not have died." When Jesus saw her weeping, and the Jews who had come with her also weeping, he was deeply moved in his spirit and greatly troubled.
John 11:32-33

The story of the resurrection of Lazarus is one of the most beautiful and awe-inspiring stories of the entire Bible. It is arguably the most incredible sign of Jesus' three-year ministry. Jesus takes a man who has literally already begun decomposing and brings his rotting and lifeless body back to life. It, in itself, is a foreshadowing of Jesus' own death, burial, and resurrection. I encourage you to read the story of Lazarus in its entirety (John 11) and glean the wonderful realities of Jesus' majestic miracle.

Mary (the sister of the deceased) experiences an understandably excruciating degree of grief and turmoil at the death of her beloved brother. However, she commits the alluring fallacy that we are all drawn to in our moments of catastrophe–the failure to trust in the provision of the Lord.

Mary falls to the feet of the Messiah with tears streaming down her face, pounds her fist into the dirt, and indirectly asks Jesus where He was in her moment of need. She wants to know why the Lord delayed in His coming while the life of her brother faded away, day after day. Mary seeks to understand why the wonderful miracles she has heard and witnessed come from the hands of the Nazarene wasn't performed upon her loving brother. Little does Mary know, she is about to see the most shocking performance she has ever experienced.

We have no right to criticize or devalue Mary for her fleshly reaction to the death of her brother, and the "late" arrival of Jesus. When we experience catastrophic events in our lives, we are tempted to do the same exact thing. "God! Where are you at?" we ask. "Jesus, why didn't you rescue me?" we question.

Believing is not seeing; for trust is believing without knowing the definite and final outcome. But our human tendencies are to lean toward the sure thing. Usually, if we cannot see an allegation unfold before us, we are hesitant to believe it could actually happen. Therefore, action is the basis for our belief as human beings. However, God does not always perform in this manner. Instead, He wishes to form you in such a way that you trust Him even when there is no action for your eyes to behold or any proof of a sure thing.

We must know and understand that God is always nearest when we are in our darkest pits of calamity (1 Peter 4:14). You must take comfort in knowing that the God of all the universe has made you a priority, and He will provide provision. It may not be the answer you are looking for, and you may experience a more intense pain than you have ever experienced, but the Savior is there, and He will come through. When you are going through the catastrophe of a lifetime, don't ask God where He is at; for if you are patient, He may roll away a stone and call out a dead man!

Day 22

The Deadman Witness

When he had said these things, he cried out with a loud voice, "Lazarus, come out." The man who had died came out, his hands and feet bound with linen strips, and his face wrapped with cloth. Jesus said to them, "Unbind him, and let him go."
John 11:43-44

Imagine watching helplessly for days as your loved one slips off into a death characterized by terrible anguish. Imagine your beloved sibling experiencing a grueling sickness, causing unimaginable amounts of pain and suffering. Imagine watching him gasp for his last breath and his life fleeting from his sickened body. Imagine seeing the undertaker wrap his dead body in linen, carry him away, place him in a tomb, and roll a stone over its entrance. Now, imagine your beloved brother, who was once defeated by illness, hop out of his tomb with his burial garb wrapped around him–by the bellowing call of the Savior.

This sight had to be unimaginably incredible for everyone who was watching; but can you imagine how indescribably baffled and overjoyed Lazarus' siblings and other family members were? I wonder if those involved in Lazarus' burial–those who wrapped him in his death cloth–were among the crowd who witnessed him peal the linen from his flesh made new. The day was etched into the memory of those who saw the resurrection of the man who was destined to die twice.

As happy and thrilled as Mary was, she had to of also felt foolhardy and ashamed. The Savior had done precisely what she had cried out and accused Him of neglecting just moments before. As happy as she must have been to see her brother again, all of her doubt in the Messiah was also wrapped up in the linen that her brother now raveled off of himself piece by piece.

At that moment, I believe a new degree of belief burst through the barriers of Mary's troublesome doubt. I think she reached a new level of intimacy with the Chosen One of God, more so than she ever had before. She may have believed Jesus was the Christ that could heal an invalid and give sight to a blind man, but now she believed in the One whom death could not conquer. Now, the grave did not have the sting upon her that it once had; for she knew that the beauties of grace overpowered the bite of death.

What about you? Do you know the Savior that intimately? I am not asking if you have been redeemed from your sin by the blood of the resurrected King. I am asking you if you are currently at a higher level of intimacy with almighty God than when He saved your wretched soul. Are you a redeemed infant, suckling on the milk of rudimentary understanding? Or are you an empowered warrior, cutting into the steak of intimacy with the Savior?

Arise doubtful Christian and behold Lazarus the dead man! Put away your bottle of immature understanding and pick up your steak knife of elevated realization. For believing in the Savior's ability to make an invalid walk will encourage you; but experiencing Him call the dead from the tomb will empower you!

Day 23

It Persists at the Feet

So they gave a dinner for him there. Martha served, and Lazarus was one of those reclining with him at table. Mary therefore took a pound of expensive ointment made from pure nard, and anointed the feet of Jesus and wiped his feet with her hair. The house was filled with the fragrance of the perfume.
John 12:2-3

Mary's journey of devotion to the Savior comes to a head at the anointing of Jesus; for she selflessly and humbly uses her resources to prepare the Messiah for burial. The life of Mary and the evolution of her belief in the Christ is depicted in three events–all involving Mary at the feet of Jesus. First, she is seen sitting at the feet of Jesus, listening to Him teach His Word (Luke 10:39). Second, she is in grave distress at the feet of the Savior, due to the death of her brother (John 11:32). Third, we find a totally devoted and transformed Mary at the feast table of the Messiah, wiping the feet of the Son of God (John 12:3).

Jesus, as He reclines at the dining table of His honorary feast, knows with perfect certainty that He is a mere six days to His death on the cross. He knows what lies ahead of Him and what must be done. Therefore, when Judas Iscariot rebukes Mary for using such expensive ointment on the feet of Jesus, He says, "Leave her alone, so that she may keep it for the day of my burial. For the poor you always have with you, but you do not always have me" (John 12:7-8). Mary and the Savior are in sync.

In chapter eleven of John, we saw the transition event in the life of Mary that took her from a nominal Christian to a mountain mover. In one chapter, she is doubting and questioning the Messiah; while in the next chapter she is wiping His dirty feet with her hair.

Something clicked in Mary that made her devoted, radical, trusting, obedient, and selfless. She transitions from a needy soul–asking from the Savior–to a giving soul that begins to sacrifice for the Savior selflessly. By the grace of Jesus Christ, Mary transitions from a miracle observer to the unstoppable force that rocked the world in the early church–a self-denying and cross-bearing warrior for the Lord. Humiliation became a given; pride became void.

When we read the story of the life of Mary, it should cause us to question the content of our lives. Are you a believer? Or are you a political Christian–someone who claims the name of Christ only to possess a heart far from the Savior?

A warrior for the Lord will give of his resources, pouring his expensive ointment upon the feet of the Messiah. A flamboyant believer will become the subject of humiliation, soiling his name with the world to advance the proclamation of Jesus Christ. A genuine Christian will deny himself and take up his cross (Luke 9:23), living entirely and fully for the Lord, regardless of the consequences.

What about you? Are you reclining devotedly and merrily at the feasting table of the Lord? Or are you glaring angrily through the window in discontent such as the Pharisees?

Day 24

Death to the King!

The next day the large crowd that had come to the feast heard that Jesus was coming to Jerusalem. So they took branches of palm trees and went out to meet him, crying out, "Hosanna! Blessed is he who comes in the name of the Lord, even the King of Israel!" And Jesus found a young donkey and sat on it, just as it is written, "Fear not, daughter Zion; behold, your king is coming, sitting on a donkey's colt!"
John 12:12-15

The triumphal entry is one of the most glorious and impactful events in the public ministry of Jesus. It is at the triumphal entry that the kingly manifestation that Jesus' own family looked so fervently for took place. The King of kings and Lord of lords strolls into His holy city as the ruler and majestic leader, fulfilling the prophecy of Zechariah 9:9. He is claiming authenticity as the Son of God and authority as the God of the ages. But how many see His imminent death looming over the horizon?

There is no doubt there were genuine believers in Christ's presence at the triumphal entry. It is apparent that many of those waving palm branches and calling, "Hosanna!" were real followers of the Christ.

However, how many fully understand the true kingship of the Messiah upon the young donkey? Does anyone truly understand what Jesus is riding into this historic city to accomplish? Is there a soul present that is prepared for the events that are to take place at the weeks end?

Why did the Pharisees reject Jesus Christ as the promised Messiah? They did not subscribe to Jesus' claims of divinity because He didn't appear as the king they were searching for. The Pharisees were not looking for a savior to save them from their sin–they denied their sin sick state. Rather, they sought a Messiah that would arise and free them from the oppression of the Roman Empire. A measly little carpenter boy from Nazareth, who had no particular excellence in appearance (Isaiah 53:2), did not fit the bill for the Pharisee's revolutionary king.

Jesus' purpose in coming to the earth as Savior was not intended to be that of revolutionary freedom and a governmental overthrow. This is why Jesus rides into Jerusalem aback a young donkey–signifying peace–rather than a mature stallion–signifying revolution. Instead, His divine purpose, as spelled out in the Old Testament, was of a more significant nature–uprising against Satan and declaring victory over death and sin.

I am interested in how many of us declare an alternative ambition upon the true purpose of Jesus in our lives. Many times, I fear that we care more about what Christ can do for *us* than what we can do for *Christ*.

Please understand that God has a sovereign and detailed plan for your life. It is not in the works of His desire for you to request approval for a designed plan of your own. Stop looking for God to start a revolution in your life. Instead, follow Him up upon the hill to Golgotha, watch Him suffocate upon a bloody tree, and behold your eyes upon the risen Savior three days later, all to fulfill the purpose of freedom.

Day 25

It Begins with the Feet

Jesus, knowing that the Father had given all things into his hands, and that he had come from God and was going back to God, rose from supper. He laid aside his outer garments, and taking a towel, tied it around his waist. Then he poured water into a basin and began to wash the disciples' feet and to wipe them with the towel that was wrapped around him.
John 13:3-5

There is no more magnificent exhibition of humility in all of history than the selfless acts of the Messiah. In a secluded upper room with His disciples, Jesus performs one of His many powerful and moving acts of humility. This, the divine King of Israel, who rode into town as the cause of a parade, now stoops down and cleanses the dirty feet of weary travelers. The Creator of the universe takes on the role of the servant, performing the duty of a hired hand.

Like what has already been suggested, cleaning the feet of the disciples would not have been a clean job. Words cannot express what a show of humility it was for the Savior to wipe the grime off of the feet of men who traveled from afar.

Further electrifying is who Jesus did not leave out of the foot washing–Judas Iscariot. Jesus did not only stoop down and wash the feet of the warriors who would spread the Gospel to the four corners of the earth; He also washed the feet of the Betrayer. How awkward it must have been for Judas as the man he would soon deliver over to the hands of the Pharisees kindly wiped the dirt from his feet. Jesus' act of humble service was not void of those who would harm Him.

It is a surreal revelation to realize that God calls us to His own perfect character. God never calls us to be something He has not always been from the beginning of time. God calls us to be perfect because He is perfect. God commands us to be loving because He is the essence of love. God demands us to exhibit true humility because He is the picturesque example of humility. God calls us to be servants because He first served us.

In addition, Jesus did not wash the feet of the disciples simply as a physical service of comfort. Instead, His act of servitude is a symbol of the coming spiritual cleansing He is to pour out upon all the elect. Just as Jesus physically wiped the dirt from the apostles' feet, He will also spiritually wipe the dirt from their hearts. Just as He poured water over their grimy feet, He will also rinse the grime from their soul.

However, as much as Jesus' foot washing is a *display* of humility and servitude, it is equally a *charge* for humility and servitude. We are to take this beautiful example of Jesus' character and form our lives to its mold. With the extravagant rewards of salvation come the clearly designed charges of servanthood. A Christian who lies back, merely watching the needs of the world, will find his complacency to be damning. The one who is genuinely in love with the Savior will have a towel wrapped around his waist.

Day 26

Characterized by Love

"A new commandment I give to you, that you love one another: just as I have loved you, you also are to love one another. By this all people will know that you are my disciples, if you have love for one another."
John 13:34-35

Jesus, viewing the cross of salvation just around the corner, breathes the summation of the law anew. As He approaches His death, Jesus wishes to leave the disciples with a new twist on an old command. "Love one another," He charges. "Just as I have loved you," He adds. The promised Messiah commands His disciples to love one another as He loved them–with selfless and sacrificial love. Just as Jesus poured Himself out as an offering, giving more than any human being ever could offer, the disciples too are to love with a giving heart–ready to selflessly sacrifice for the benefit of others.

Jesus claims that by the outward appearance of humble love, the world will know that they are of Him. By displaying a type of love that is so contrary to the world, the world will know where, and with whom, the follower in Christ stands. No other force or emotion is more distinguishing than that of the sacrificial love of Christ.

It is a shame that the world is far more aware of what we are against than what we are for as Christians. Many times, well-intentioned believers crank up the heat on lost and rebellious souls in the name of moral rebuke, leaving love far behind. Scripture does command rebuke on a wayward brother, but it does not permit a rebuke of hate. On the contrary, the apostle Peter declares that we are to be ready to defend the Gospel with *gentleness* and *respect* (1 Peter 3:15). We are to proclaim the truth with the spark of tenderness and with the fuel of love.

The world is not to declare us Christian just because we claim Christ's name, but because our lives consist of the fire and electricity of Christ's love! Just as Jesus spent the majority of His time displaying love rather than speaking of it, we too ought to back up our words of love threefold with actions. Jesus masterfully created disciples of action, not empty talk.

I invite you to honestly evaluate your life regarding the command Jesus gave His disciples. If we are going to claim the lineage of the Savior, we must perform the duties due to a son or daughter of the King. If we dare to call ourselves sons or daughters of the King, we must walk worthy of His Gospel (Philippians 1:27). If we are to walk worthy of His calling, we must sacrificially love as the Savior loved.

Be honest with yourself. Are you loving like Jesus–humbling offering sacrifices for the benefit of others? Or are you hateful like the world–selfishly seeking to obtain from others?

Day 27

To Dwell with the Savior

"Let not your hearts be troubled. Believe in God; believe also in me. In my Father's house are many rooms. If it were not so, would I have told you that I go to prepare a place for you? And if I go and prepare a place for you, I will come again and will take you to myself, that where I am you may be also."
John 14:1-3

In the midst of "bad" news, Jesus offers the disciples a word of encouragement and cheer. He tells that among His chosen disciples someone would betray Him, and Peter would deny Him, yet He encourages, "Let not your heart be troubled." Jesus eases their hearts and minds by declaring that though He would leave for a time, in order to prepare them a place, He would certainly come again and bring them to Himself.

In ancient Jewish culture, the bridegroom would build onto the family home for the bride to be. When the bridegroom completed the construction of the addition, the bridegroom would come, marry his bride, and bring her home. Jesus certainly drew upon this cultural tradition.

As children of God, we wait as the Lord prepares a room in the house of the Father. The reunion of Jesus and His disciples–at the second coming–will be that of a family reunion, with all the members of the family coming to live and dwell together forever.

Heaven will not be a place with thousands of separate individual houses holding the children of God separately. Instead, it will be a glorious place of family gathering in one central home, with the Lord sitting at the head of the table. We will live, eat, and be merry together, as God sovereignly designed.

The wonders and beauties of heaven would be nothing but rubbish without the Savior. The crystal sea would be as good as a murky cesspool if the Lord were not there. The streets of Gold might as well be tarnished without the footsteps of Jesus upon them. The pearly gates would be as fake counterfeits without the glory of the Lord shining upon them. Without God, heaven would not be all that it is cracked up to be.

What is your desire? Does the content of your desire rest with the joys and possession of Jesus Christ? Or does your desire consist of only self-preservation? Why do you want to go to heaven? Do you wish to go so you may live and dwell with the Lord? Or do you wish to go to partake only of the riches and amenities that heaven includes? Do you wish to go to your eternal home to praise and worship the Savior forever? Or do you want to to go only to escape the fiery clutches of hell?

Please remember, Satan would very much like to dwell in heaven and avoid his eternal punishment. However, his desire to be heavenly isn't because he wishes to glorify and honor the Savior. If you are satisfied with a heaven void of the Savior, heaven will be void of you.

Day 28

Experiencing the Helper

"If you love me, you will keep my commandments. And I will ask the Father, and he will give you another Helper, to be with you forever, even the Spirit of Truth, whom the world cannot receive, because it neither sees him nor knows him. You know him, for he dwells with you and will be in you."
John 14:15-17

Here, as Jesus conducts one of His last conversations with His disciples, He promises and declares the third person of the Godhead–the Holy Spirit. He calls the Holy Spirit another Helper that will be with and within the disciples. He will help them, strengthen them, guide them, and bring remembrance to their minds of the things they seen and heard from the hands and lips of Jesus. This new era in the disciples' lives would be one of empowerment, by the implantation of the teachings and miracles of Jesus into their hearts.

The Holy Spirit is the most mystifying person of the Godhead; even Christians struggle to understand the implications of Him. This should make sense since Jesus makes it clear that the world will not receive Him because it lacks the ability to see Him or know Him. The more we are ingrained in the world, the less we will see the beautiful wonders of the Holy Spirit and know His majesty and power. It isn't until we gravitate toward godliness that His elements and aspects begin to take shape in our hearts and minds.

We are quick to criticize the disciples of their lack of faith and abundance of doubt pre-ascension. However, though no sufficient excuse is to be made for questioning the thoughts and actions of our Lord, we must also understand that they did not possess the power of the Holy Spirit that we so often neglect. Their lives and decisions did not contain the tug and pull of the knowledge, strength, and guidance of the intimate manifestation of the Spirit. Though they did have God in His physical form (Jesus) to teach and instruct them in righteousness, they were void of the far more personal implantation of the Helper. We as 21st century Christians, on the other hand, have a far stricter responsibility for righteousness than the disciples of Jesus pre-ascension.

The Holy Spirit is where we obtain life, sanctification, guidance, knowledge, and salvation. Where do you stand with the Holy Spirit? Is He a foreign concept to you that you have yet to see or know? Is He a faint idea to you that has little impact on how you live and interact with others? Does the Holy Spirit set you on fire for the mission of Jesus Christ, enabling you to perform acts of God that change and transform lives supernaturally?

Ask God to fill you with His Holy Spirit. Ask God to saturate you with an exuberant desire for His powerful and inspiring Spirit. The farther you drift into the clutches of the world, the less you will know and experience the Spirit. What are your experiences?

Day 29

Pruning for the Harvest

"I am the vine; you are the branches. Whoever abides in me and I in him, he it is that bears much fruit, for apart from me you can do nothing. If anyone does not abide in me he is thrown away like a branch and withers; and the branches are gathered, thrown into the fire, and burned."
John 15:5-6

Pruning is an essential aspect of reaping great rewards from your planted seed. Water and nutrients flow up the stem of the plant and distribute the needed ingredients of life to each bulb. Therefore, you prune away some of the bulbs of the plant to provide the largest and most productive bulbs with the most nutrients possible, in order to reap a greater harvest. Naturally, the bulbs that are withered and unproductive would be pruned off in an effort to abstain from wasting nutrients.

Jesus uses this illustration here when He compares Himself to the vine and the disciples to the branches. If the branches abide in the vine, they will produce much fruit. However, if they do not abide in the vine, they are pruned off and gathered up to be thrown into the fire.

We are not saved by the good deeds or selfless acts of service we perform as Christians, but good deeds and selfless service is no doubt an essential aspect of the Christian religion. James says,

> What good is it, my brothers, if someone says he has faith but does not have works? Can that faith save him? If a brother or sister is poorly clothed and lacking daily food, and one of you says to them, 'Go in peace, be warmed and filled,' without giving them the things needed for the body, what good is that? So also faith by itself, if it does not have works, is dead." (James 2:14-17).

Our good works, as Christians, are produced by our gracious and merciful salvation.

If a man does not view the enormity of the grace of his salvation, and if he neglects to work and produce for the Lord that saved his soul, his salvation should come into question. For though our works are not the *cause* of our salvation, works are the *result* of our salvation. To neglect doing heavenly deeds for God's glory is to overlook the fruit of salvation. Those who do neglect to bear fruit, Jesus says He will prune off and cast into the fire.

Just as Jesus declares the uselessness of salt that loses its saltiness and proclaims that it is worthy for nothing but to be trampled on by men (Matthew 5:13), so too, is the branch that lacks to show any whim of fruit-bearing. The tasteless salt and the unproductive branch hold the same fate–hellfire and gnashing of the teeth.

Is your life a result of the selfless works of Christ? Or is your life a result of the selfish works of yourself? Jesus said that if you abide in Him, you will exhibit works of righteousness. Will you be harvested? Or will you be gathered?

Day 30

For More than Jewels

"If the world hates you, know that it has hated me before it hated you. If you were of the world, the world would love you as its own; but because you are not of the world, but I chose you out of the world, therefore the world hates you. Remember the word that I said to you: 'A servant is not greater than his master.' If they persecuted me, they will also persecute you."
John 15:18-20

It should never catch us off guard when the world acts worldly. It should never surprise us when sinful people behave in an immoral manner. It is easy for Christians to get wrapped up in deciphering and lamenting over the travesties of the world. It should never shock the children of God when the world launches an all-out assault upon Christianity. The world has persecuted believers from the very beginning of time. It should be a firm understanding that those who call themselves Christians will be slandered, ridiculed, and persecuted by the world.

Jesus plainly warns his disciples on many occasions of the persecution they are to endure for the name and glory of Christ. Every disciple, with the exception of John, died a rather horrific death–due to proclaiming the name of Jesus. Even John didn't gain luxury for speaking the Gospel; he was banished to a lonely island. The apostle Paul–the most quoted man in history, having written a large portion of the New Testament–was arguably the most persecuted of them all (read 2 Corinthians 11:24-27 to hear of his accounts of persecution).

We should scorn those who guarantee nothing but bliss and luxury for converting to Christianity. The Bible does not teach that fallacy but teaches quite the contrary. The greatest men of the Bible are namely those who were persecuted the most. Yes, God blesses his children, but it is not in materialistic avenues of luxury that make it harder to reach heaven. For Jesus said, "Truly, I say to you, only with difficulty will a rich person enter the kingdom of heaven. Again I tell you, it is easier for a camel to go through the eye of a needle than for a rich person to enter the kingdom of heaven" (Matthew 19:23-24). Surely God would not bless his warriors with something that would drive a wedge between them and Himself.

The point is not that God doesn't bless His children with material things; He does from time to time. However, becoming a Christian for material blessings will not only be non-genuine; it will also be terribly disappointing.

We, as Americans, live in the safest place in the world to be a Christian; but we will experience persecution for the sake of Christ. Wherever the world (non-believers) is, no matter how safe the atmosphere may seem; persecution is sure to come for the believer. This does not mean that we should live in fear or negativity; but that we should be ready and alert for the ridicule and shame that is coming our way. True believers in Christ will persevere until the end. Will you?

Day 31

He was Emptied so that I may be Filled

"When the Spirit of truth comes, he will guide you into all the truth, for he will not speak on his own authority, but whatever he hears he will speak, and he will declare to you the things that are to come. He will glorify me, for he will take what is mine and declare it to you."
John 16:13-14

Imagine the state of confusion the disciples were in as Jesus spoke of His departure from this world. A few verses earlier He tells them, "Nevertheless, I tell you the truth: it is to your advantage that I go away, for if I do not go away, the Helper will not come to you. But if I go, I will send him to you" (John 16:7). This man, whom they have witnessed give sight to the blind, provide strength to the crippled, raise the dead from the grave, and prove Himself as the Son of God, is now claiming He will depart from them for their benefit. Surely, we can understand and empathize with their sorrow and confusion. However, their sorrow and confusion would be laid to rest when they came face to face with the promised Holy Spirit.

The first thing I want us to see about the Holy Spirit is that the Holy Spirit is a living breathing Being, not an object. Many times, we lull into the bad habit of using the word "it" with the Holy Spirit, as if He were merely an item. The Holy Spirit is God Himself–the Creator of the universe and Mediator of sins. When Jesus says that He is going away from His disciples, He simply means that God incarnate (Jesus) will go away. This is not to suggest that there is to be no article of God found among them.

We must plaster it into our hearts and minds that the Holy Spirit, Jesus, and God the Father are all one God. We are not polytheistic–meaning we worship multiple Gods.[7] We are monotheistic–meaning we worship one God.[8]

However, throughout time and space our one God has shown Himself in three forms–God the Father (Creator), God the Son (Jesus), and God the Spirit (the Holy Spirit). When God the Creator breathed life into the nostrils of Adam, He pulled oxygen from the lungs of the Son and breathed it out from the lips of the Spirit. They are all one God.

What makes this truth so magnificent is realizing that when we receive the Holy Spirit of God, we obtain the same life-giving power that was used to raise Jesus Christ from the grave (Romans 8:11). It is the Spirit that makes us righteous, blameless, and perfect. When you become the temple of the Holy Spirit (1 Corinthians 6:19), the Creator of the universe dwells within you.

---

[7] Dictionary.com defines "polytheism" as, "the doctrine of or belief in more than one god or in many gods." https://www.dictionary.com/browse/polytheism, accessed September 22, 2018.

[8] Dictionary.com defines "monotheism" as, "the doctrine or belief that there is only one God." https://www.dictionary.com/browse/monotheism?s=t, accessed September 22, 2018.

With this realization comes immense power and great responsibility. The Spirit is the reason many signs and wonders were performed by the apostles of the early church. The Spirit is the reason for tongues of fire and prophecy. Those filled with the Spirit performed unexplainable acts for the glory of the Lord, moving the world toward the understanding of Jesus. What about you? Are you filled?

Day 32

Ask for Delight in Me

> "So also you have sorrow now, but I will see you again, and your hearts will rejoice, and no one will take your joy from you. In that day you will ask nothing of me. Truly, truly, I say to you, whatever you ask of the Father in my name, he will give it to you. Until now you have asked nothing in my name. Ask, and you will receive, that your joy may be full."
> John 16:22-24

This is the last full structured conversation Jesus has with the assembly of His disciples before He is betrayed into the hands of the Jews. In chapter seventeen, we have Jesus' prayer; and in chapter eighteen we have His betrayal. Once again, He is ensuring the disciples of the joy in the Holy Spirit they will experience after He has departed. When they receive the Holy Spirit at Pentecost, their hearts will overflow with a pleasure no man, beast, or evil spirit can take away from them; for they will be closer to the Almighty than ever before.

When Jesus was alive on earth with His disciples, they physically had to approach the Messiah and make a request of Him. After the ascension and the indwelling of the Holy Spirit, Jesus tells them this handicap will no longer exist. When the Holy Spirit enters into a person, that person can then approach the heavenly

Father more intimately in prayer–to make requests in the name of Jesus.

But what does it mean to ask for something in the name of Jesus Christ? This does not mean that material requests can be made to the Father for luxurious gain only. When Psalm 37 says, "Delight yourself in the LORD, and he will give you the desires of your heart" (Psalm 37:4), it does not mean God will give you every lust of material wealth and prosperity that your mind possesses. The verse before and after Psalm 37:4 concerns trust and commitment to the LORD! When I delight in the LORD, I will no longer lust for the evil things of this world; and material items will no longer compete for the love of my heart. When I delight in the LORD, the LORD will indeed give me the desires of my heart–more of Himself!

Unfortunately, too many times we attempt to use God as a genie-in-a-bottle to grant all of our frivolous wishes. We request cars, money, promotions, etc. and tag a little "In Jesus Name" on end to make it official. This is not honoring to God, and in many instances, it is blasphemous and heretical.

When we give or perform something in the name of someone here on earth, it would be dishonoring to do it toward an act or a cause that they would not support or approve. When we ask something in the name of the Son, it ought to have first been discerned and declared the will of God. Do not formulate your own plans and ask them in Jesus' name. As Christians, our lives, attitudes, and decisions ought to be saturated with Jesus.

The more Christlike you become, the more your desires will be fulfilled. This is because your desires are that of the Messiah, and His will certainly will be done.

Invite the Holy Spirit to fill your soul and sanctify you. Invite Him to align your desires with His holiness and greatness. When your heart is on the same page as God's, your desires will be fulfilled, your requests will be made, and your joy will be unquenchable.

Day 33

The Everlasting Intentions of Glory

"Father, the hour has come; glorify your Son that the Son may glorify you, since you have given him authority over all flesh, to give eternal life to all whom you have given him. And this is eternal life, that they know you the only true God, and Jesus Christ whom you have sent. I glorified you on earth, having accomplished the work that you gave me to do. And now, Father, glorify me in your own presence with the glory that I had with you before the world existed."
John 17:1-5

In John chapter seventeen, we receive the most excellent prayer ever uttered from human lips: the High Priestly Prayer. Jesus–the God of all the universe–spends time alone with the Father, to bring all that has happened and all that will be completed to a head. I urge you to spend time in this chapter of prayer and contemplate the sacrifice of our Savior as tears roll down your face. The character, divinity, and agenda of Jesus Christ is wholly summed up in this one short chapter in John. This is our Savior's prayer.

The first reality I hope for us to glean from this prayer is the divinity and everlasting presence of Jesus Christ. There has never been a moment inside of time or outside of time when Jesus did not exist. He always has been and forever will be; for He and the Father are one. We first approached this truth at the beginning of our journey through the Gospel of John (see Day 1) where Scripture says, "In the beginning was the Word, and the Word was with God, and the Word was God" (John 1:1). Now, we have the same claim charged by the Word itself: "And now, Father, glorify me in your presence with the glory that I had with you before the world existed" (vs. 5). Jesus Christ is divine, and Jesus Christ is eternal.

We do not serve a new and namby-pamby God. We do not trust in the authority of a revolutionary liar, that only recently thrust himself onto the scene. Instead, we serve and believe in the crucifixion, burial, resurrection, and forgiveness of the One who separated the clouds from the seas who and planted the beautiful garden in Eden.

The second reality that I hope for us to glean from this prayer is the radical and persistent humility of the Savior. This is the God of Israel, who possesses the power of a lion, coming to His people with the meekness of a lamb. Jesus was born by humble means, served by humble means, prayed by humble means, and died by humble means. There is not a sliver of the essence of pride within the Messiah, and He humbly shows it. Though He asks for glorification, His glory is but a platform to glorify the Father.

How much of what you do is for the glorification of the Father? If the singer sings a beautiful melody–in an effort to draw ears and eyes upon herself–her talent is but a waste of sound waves. If the preacher preaches inspiring words of wisdom and eloquence–in an effort to produce awe and praise upon himself – his preaching is but a waste of words. We must live our lives with the intention of glorifying the Glorifier. What's your intention?

Day 34

Joy in the Father

"While I was with them, I kept them in your name, which you have given me. I have guarded them, and not one of them has been lost except the son of destruction, that the scripture might be fulfilled. But now I am coming to you, and these things I speak in the world, that they may have my joy fulfilled in themselves."
John 17:12-13

One of the greatest tragedies of those who do not submit to the saving graces of our Lord is their lack of joy in the Messiah. To consecrated believers in Christ, the idea of living outside of the joy of the Father is foreign and bizarre. When we find ourselves saved by the graces of God and transformed by the invasion of the Holy Spirit, we gain a fulfilling joy that is surpassed by no sensation in all of existence. It is a joy that not even the gates of hell may destroy.

Here, in Jesus' High Priestly prayer, we see His merciful purposes in leaving the luxuries of heaven to enter a cold and dark world. Jesus' purpose in coming as the promised Messiah was to obediently fulfill the sovereign plan of the Father–to rescue and redeem wayward sinners.

His exhibition of humility and sacrifice was for our profit of adoption and joy. For those who were once regarded heathenistic and deemed damned and deplorable, Jesus died so that they might be considered to be holy and deemed righteous and shameless. He miraculously descended, humbly served, sacrificially died, victoriously resurrected, and remarkably ascended, so that we would have His joy fulfilled in us. But what is this joy that has been achieved in those of us who have been entrusted to the Savior?

Christ's joy is what enables a Christian to walk, talk, and behave as a Christian. It is Christ's joy, implanted by the Holy Spirit, that constitutes and enacts transformation in a heart made of stone. It is Christ's joy that turns bitter misery into refreshing relief. It is Christ's joy that alters a heart of lustful desires into a vessel of content satisfaction. It is Christ's joy that converts an evil disposition to that of righteousness.

It is this joy, graciously given by the Father, that conditions us to delight in the Lord, resulting in the desires of our heart (Psalm 37:4). When we are filled with the joy of Christ, it not only makes our trials and tribulations bearable, but it also makes them embracive! The joy of the Lord makes sin utterly repulsive and righteousness ferociously enticing.

Where do you land in the joy of the Lord? The more we grow in the joy of Christ, the more we emulate Christ. Maybe your life is missing an unspeakably full joy that would put all the puzzle pieces together. Take a step of faith, and take the hand of the Savior so you may have joy in the Father.

Day 35

Stop and Dirty Your Knee

"I do not ask for these only, but also for those
who will believe in me through their word,
that they may all be one, just as you, Father,
are in me, and I in you, that they also may be
in us, so that the world may believe that you
have sent me."
John 17:20-21

This may be the most humbling and sobering passage in all of the Bible. Our Lord and Savior–the Maker who created the stars in the heavens and the oxygen in the air–took the time to kneel, dirty His knee, and pray for you and me. He did not reserve His time in prayer with the Father to only the fold of the Israelites; He extended His petition for fulfillment also to the Gentiles–you and me. Just as He did not withhold His salvation from the pagan Gentiles, His prayers, too, He did not withhold.

Further humbling, is the realization of what consisted of Jesus' prayer. He asked for our preservation of the evil one–that Satan may not overtake us with his power of destruction and deceit. He asked for our sanctification in truth–to be made holy, blameless and perfect. He gave us a sacred mission–to be sent into the world to proclaim the most excellent news known to the universe. Jesus consecrated Himself for our sake so that we may be sanctified in truth.

I believe that no man may honestly and righteously declare his prayer life to be at the degree of excellence that it should. We, as fallen creatures, will continually struggle to adequately commune with our Lord until the day we meet Him in the air, and perfect communication is restored between creation and Creator. However, great strides can, and should, be taken to etch away at the divide in conversation from the mortal to the Immortal. We have a responsibility to desire a more intimate dialogue with the Almighty.

Prayer is a gracious and remarkable privilege from God to His children that we dare not neglect. Prayer in itself is a wild suggestion. To suppose that we have a direct number to the Maker of light would seem bizarre and unbelievable. However, God provided far more than a direct line; He drew us unto Himself!

How often do you pray? Satan's number one tool in separating you from the most marvelous privilege known to man is to convince you that your schedule is more important than your direct link with the Savior.

Do not become too busy to perform the single most enriching duty of all the universe. Jesus–the Master and Savior–knelt down, dirtied His knee, and halted his ministerial endeavors to speak to the Father. If the Savior felt the need to pray, shouldn't you?

Day 36

The Voice of Truth

Then Pilate said to him, "So you are a king?" Jesus answered, "You say that I am a king. For this purpose I was born and for this purpose I have come into the world – to bear witness to the truth. Everyone who is of the truth listens to my voice. Pilate said to him, "What is truth?"
John 18:37-38

We have come to the beginning of the dreaded outcome of the Gospel of John–the death of our Savior. However, as dreaded as it is to read of the false accusations, the lashes on his back, the nails that were driven into His wrists, and His asphyxiation on the cross, it is also a wonderful cumulation of joy and gratitude. For we know that the story does not end with his suffocation on the cross, but in his glorious resurrection from the dead. And by his defeat of death, we may have eternal life.

Jesus had been betrayed by one of His own disciples–Judas Iscariot–and dragged to the court of Pilate after being falsely accused by the Jews. Pilate, attempting to understand the case for death to this man of peace, asks, "Are you the King of the Jews?" (John 18:33). He asks this question not merely for the purpose of clarification, but also to find grounds for a political charge. Jesus clarifies that His kingship is not a revolutionary kingship on earth, with the goal of taking charge of the politics of Israel, but rather a kingship of another world–a kingship of heaven that bears witness to the truth.

Then, Pilate asks one of the most significant questions in all of the universe. He asks, "What is truth?" (vs. 8). In Pilate's question, you see a ray of interest, an abundance of mysticism and skepticism, and an earnest desire to understand. He asks a question that has blasted from the hearts of men since the dawn of time. He asks a question with an answer that resolves all confusion and miscommunication. What is truth?

In our postmodern world, we live in a day of subjectivity. That is, the essence of truth is found in my own evaluation and opinion of what truth is. In other words, you decide what truth is for you and I will decide what truth is for me. It charges that we must be tolerant of different individual views of truth, even if it conflicts with our own since truth is subjective and can change.

Please abhor the heretical and unbiblical claims of our postmodern culture concerning the subjectivity of truth. I plead that you would refuse to compromise and conform to the ideas of truth composed by the simple concepts of man. Instead, wrap your arms around the truth of the Scriptures, and embrace it for what it is– the ultimate and infallible truth of God!

We need not tire ourselves over deciphering and searching for the ultimate truth; for it is found in the 66 objective books of the Bible. Jesus Christ is the essence of truth, and His truth is not subjectively contingent upon my opinion or any other opinion. We may celebrate the truths of Scripture for its revealing accounts of Jesus Christ; for it plainly answers Pilate's question.

When Pilate asked, "What *is* truth?" (emphasis added) he was ignorantly unaware that he was staring into the very face *of* truth.

Day 37

To Ordain Thy Death for Thee

He entered his headquarters again and said to Jesus, "Where are you from?" But Jesus gave him no answer. So Pilate said to him, "You will not speak to me? Do you not know that I have authority to release you and authority to crucify you?" Jesus answered him, "You would have no authority over me at all unless it had been given you from above. Therefore he who delivered me over to you has the greater sin."
John 19:9-11

When the Jew's fruitless attempt to accuse Jesus of a political crime–alleging He declared Himself King (in the revolutionary sense)–fell through, they then began charging Him with a religious crime–declaring Himself the Son of God. Understand that the Jews are correct in condemning a man to death for blaspheming God. By Mosaic law, if a man declares himself to be God, he is to be put to death. Therefore, Jesus should rightly and legally be put to death if He professes to be the Diviner unless He is in fact, God!

So, at the boisterous cries of the Jewish leaders, Pilate takes Jesus back into his headquarters for the second time for understanding and counsel. Pilate, intelligent enough to know Jesus is no ordinary man, yet skeptical and foolish enough not to recognize His divine authority, asks Him where He is from. When Jesus refuses to answer his question, Pilate indeed shows his ignorance by asserting that he has full power to decide Jesus' fate. Jesus reminds this naïve governing figure that the authority that he possesses was given to him from the Almighty–namely the man he is about to sentence to death.

What is staggering about this occurrence is that Jesus' death is entirely and wholly voluntary. Jesus tells Peter in the garden of Gethsemane when he attempts to deliver Him from his arrest, "Do you think that I cannot appeal to my Father, and he will at once send me more than twelve legions of angels?" (Matthew 26:53). Jesus had full authority and capability to deliver Himself from His bloody and miserable fate.

However, He has such an obsessed passion and love for us that He willingly was wrongfully accused, disrespectfully slapped, blatantly mocked, brutally flogged, and inhumanely crucified. He sovereignly ordained Golgotha for the redemption of you and me.

We owe all that we are and all that we will be to the blood-soaked Savior that was strung up between two criminals. For it is He that grasped our wretched ankles and pulled us from the black hole of depravity. No amount of righteous living can replace the outstanding act of redemption upon the cross that resulted in the atonement of sin.

Jesus willingly gave up His spirit to purposefully fulfill yours. What have you given for Him? What have you nailed to the cross for His kingdom? Just as the old hymn sings, "I gave, I gave My life for thee, What hast thou giv'n for Me?"[9]

---

[9] Francis R. Havergal, "I Gave My Life for Thee," 1858.

Day 38

The Climax of History

So they took Jesus, and he went out, bearing his own cross, to the place called The Place of a Skull, which in Aramaic is called Golgotha. There they crucified him, and with two others, one on either side, and Jesus beside them. Pilate also wrote an inscription and put it on the cross. It read, "Jesus of Nazareth, the King of the Jews."
John 19:16-19

We finally arrive at the climax of all history and future events–Jesus Christ's crucifixion. Literally, every man's fate hinges upon this event and the result of it three days later. Families have been broken, lives have been shattered, and heads have been taken on account of where a man stands on this real and historical occurrence. There is no doubt that Jesus was crucified on Golgotha in Jerusalem–it is an accurate and historical fact. The division lies not in whether He died, but for what means He died for and whether or not He miraculously arose.

Did Jesus die simply as an unfortunate subject of His time? Or did He die as the true Son of God for the redemption of the world? Be careful, the answer to these questions will cost you.

The cross was a brutal means of public humiliation and physical torture. The Gospel of John gives one of the vaguest accounts of the crucifixion. Jesus, having been be beaten to within an inch of His life, abandoned by almost everyone He loved and forced to carry a heavy wooden cross up a hill, was then strung up naked on that cross to suffocate. He, who committed no crime, was placed between two criminals. He was mocked and cursed by those who urged He was an imposter.

Jesus became the face of *our* defilement so that we could become the face of *His* preservation. "For our sake he made him to be sin who knew no sin, so that in him we might become the righteousness of God" (2 Corinthians 5:21).

If you will, I implore you to take some time out of your day and contemplate what Jesus did upon the cross of Calvary. Sympathize with the humiliation of being strung up on a wooden beam, while everyone stared at your exposed and naked body. Imagine the heartbreak of being abandoned by those whom you love in your weakest and darkest hour, while your own people mocked and ridiculed you.

Understand that while the physical torture of lifting Himself up from the nails to gain His next breath–bearing all His weight on His punctured wounds–was excruciatingly painful, it was no match for the torment of becoming the detestable picture of sin to the Father. Paint a picture for yourself of the love Jesus had for you even before you were even conceived.

I urge you to read the crucifixion scenes of all the Gospels (Matthew 27; Mark 15; Luke 23; John 19). Read these crucifixion accounts as if you have never read them before. Weep as though you were totally unaware of what the Messiah endured for your redemption. Allow your numbness of Jesus' crucifixion to melt away, leaving you with a raw and intense passion for his sacrifice. Never forget that your salvation was expensive, and its implications for your life are colossal.

Day 39

The Risen King

On the evening of that day, the first day of the week, the doors being locked where the disciples were for fear of the Jews, Jesus came and stood among them and said to them, "Peace be with you." When he had said this, he showed them his hands and his side. Then the disciples were glad when they saw the Lord.
John 20:19-20

Imagine the Messiah your culture and society has awaited the arrival of for hundreds of years personally picked you out to follow Him in His ministry. Contemplate how wonderful it would be to cast your eyes upon the Savior as He gave strength to the crippled, sight to the blind, and the miracle of life to the dead. Envision the revelation He would create in you by explaining the many questions of your existence. Conceptualize the pure force of experiencing a supernaturally radical and selfless love that filled the depths of your heart and soul like nothing you have experienced before. Imagine physically experiencing Jesus Christ–the Savior of the world.

Now, contemplate–in light of the exuberating three years you have just spent with Him–glaring at the bloody cross your hero died upon. Fathom the sheer terror and disappointment of watching the Savior of your dreams find His demise upon a Roman cross. The disciples were in a state of desperation and devastation.

The disciples were in a precarious situation–their mystifying hero had been killed, they had all scattered, and now the Jews were after them. They had their doors barred shut and locked as they secretly met; for the fiery ordeal of persecution had already begun (1 Peter 4:12). In a state of confusion and disbelief, they were unsure of what to do next. And then the Savior was before them!

When He showed them His nail-scarred hands and His pierced side, confusion transformed to certainty and disbelief was repented to faith. Many have said the followers of Jesus did not truly witness the resurrected Christ–that it was a mere hallucination. However, to those such as the disciples who have been unveiled to the truth, only one reality is certain–resurrection!

You and I do not serve and celebrate the bones of a once great king. We serve the living God of Abraham, Isaac, Jacob, and Moses! Yes, Jesus hung on a rugged cross–exposed for the whole world to see and mock, and to become the subject of sin and shame–but we mustn't forget the morning and evening of the first day of the week, lest we forget the resurrection.

When Jesus took the wrath of God and was banished to a cold grave, He took with him sin, depravity, and death itself. And though He brought shame, scorn, and sin with Him to the grave, nothing but power, glory, and majesty accompanied Him at the resurrection. My sin can be put to death because He lives! "Because He lives, I can face tomorrow; Because He lives all fear is gone; Because I know He holds the future, And life is worth the living just because He lives."[10]

---

[10] Gloria Gaither and William J. Gaither, "Because He Lives," 1971.

Day 40

The Restoration

He said to him the third time, "Simon, son of John, do you love me?" Peter was grieved because he said to him the third time, "Do you love me?" and he said to him, "Lord, you know everything; you know that I love you." Jesus said to him, "Feed my sheep."
John 21:17

Jesus never spoke a frivolous word in His life, nor did He so much as utter a purposeless sound during His earthly inhabitation. He neither will do so in the future nor did He in the past. What Jesus has said, says, or will say will always be genuine and will forever come to pass. Therefore, He commands the same out of us. If we declare that we will do something, we are to do it. Furthermore, God will forever be more pleased and more impressed with our actions than with our declarations. However, the apostle Peter did not possess a good track record in this department early on.

Jesus, in His omniscience, declared Peter's threefold denial of Him in the garden of Gethsemane.

With a spirit of fervency Peter exclaims, "Though they all fall away because of you, I will never fall away" (Matthew 26:33).

Jesus, knowing better, says to him, "Truly, I tell you, this very night, before the rooster crows, you will deny me three times" (Matthew 26:34).

With a lack of knowledge concerning the events of the future, Peter replies to Jesus' declaration, "Even if I must die with you, I will not deny you!" (Matthew 26:35). Unfortunately, Peter does indeed deny Jesus three times; but the story does not end there.

In John 21, we have what is called "the restoration of Peter." Jesus asks Peter three times if he loves Him–in response to Peter's threefold denial of Christ. In asking Peter if he loves Him three times, Jesus is driving home to Peter the emptiness of useless words and the weightiness of significant action. Each time Peter declares his love for the Savior, He says, "Feed my Lambs" or "Tend my sheep" or "Feed my sheep" (John 21:15-17). The Great Shepherd was illustrating to Peter that love is accompanied by, and facilitated through, the care and love for the flock. A *declaration* of love is fruitless and void unless it consists of a *display* of love.

It is a lie to suggest that you love Christ so much you will lay your life down for His name's sake unless you are willing to actively do just that. In Jesus' restoration of Peter, Jesus creates for Himself a warrior that would do just that. He says of Peter, "When you are old, you will stretch out your hands, and another will dress you and carry you where you do not want to go" (John 21:18). Swiftly, the denier becomes dedicated.

Please understand that God does not want namby-pamby Christians who declare empty and frivolous promises. He wants warriors that will endure, persevere, and thrive in a world that scorns His cause and

His name. The world is not impressed and attracted to the Gospel when we make lofty declarations. Instead, the world is influenced and drawn to the Gospel when the Gospel is radically and supernaturally lived out before their eyes.

It is essential that you refrain from using your Christian name simply and only as a pretty badge; but instead, use your adoption into the holy family as a means to actively escalate the cause for Christ. Don't just proclaim whims of God's magnificent glory; live it!

Selected Bibliography

Erdman, Charles R. *An Exposition: The Gospel of John.* Philadelphia: The Westminster Press, 1929.

Foxe, John. *Foxe's Christian Martyrs of the World.* Ulrichsville: Barbour Publishing Inc.

Gaither, Gloria, and William J. Gaither. "Because He Lives." 1971.

Havergal, Francis R. "I Gave My Life for Thee." 1858

https://www.dictionary.com/browse/monotheism?s=t, (accessed September 22, 2018).

https://www.dictionary.com/browse/polytheism, (accessed September 22, 2018).

http://www.etymonline.com/word/boanerges, (accessed July, 15, 2018).

Lipka, Micheal. "Americans' faith in God may be eroding." http://www.pewresearch.org/fact-tank/2015/11/04/americans-faith-in-god-may-be-eroding/ (accessed July 4, 2018).

Piper, John. https://twitter.com/johnpiper/status/836924308505133058?lang=en (accessed July 4, 2018).

Smith Jr, Robert. *Doctrine that Dances: Bringing Doctrinal Preaching and Teaching to Life.* Nashville: B&H Publishing Group, 2008.

Printed in Poland
by Amazon Fulfillment
Poland Sp. z o.o., Wrocław